CHESTER TO BIRKENHEAD

Vic Mitchell and Keith Smith

MP Middleton Press

Front cover: With the leading coach gleaming, 2-6-4T no. 42613 stands at Hooton with the 2.45pm Birkenhead Woodside to Paddington on 20th August 1966. An express locomotive will couple to the other end of the train at Chester and no. 42613 will perform another local task. (H.Ballantyne)

Back cover upper: The much admired terminus at Birkenhead Woodside was photographed on 8th August 1962. Blowing off is 2-6-4T no. 42212, which is about to leave at 8.50am with the Paddington coaches, destined for Chester in its charge. (E.Wilmshurst)

Back cover lower: Minutes later, we look in the other direction and witness a train emerging from the tunnel, while ex-LMS 0-6-0T no. 47372 backs towards the smoke filled cutting. The location was atmospheric in several senses. (E.Wilmshurst)

Published June 2012

ISBN 978 1 908174 21 5

Design Deborah Esher

Published by
Middleton Press
Easebourne Lane
Midhurst
West Sussex
GU29 9AZ
Tel: 01730 813169
Fax: 01730 812601
Email: info@middletonpress.co.uk
www.middletonpress.co.uk

Printed in the United Kingdom by Henry Ling Limited, at the Dorset Press, Dorchester, DT1 1HD

INDEX

ACKNOWLEDGEMENTS

We are very grateful for the assistance received from many of those mentioned in the credits, also to B.Bennett, A.R.Carder, G.Croughton, S.C.Jenkins, F.Hornby, N.Langridge, B.Lewis, J.P.McCrickard, S.Ralston (Merseyrail), Mr S. and Dr S.Salter, T.Walsh and in particular, our always supportive wives, Barbara Mitchell and Janet Smith.

1. Route map in 1947.

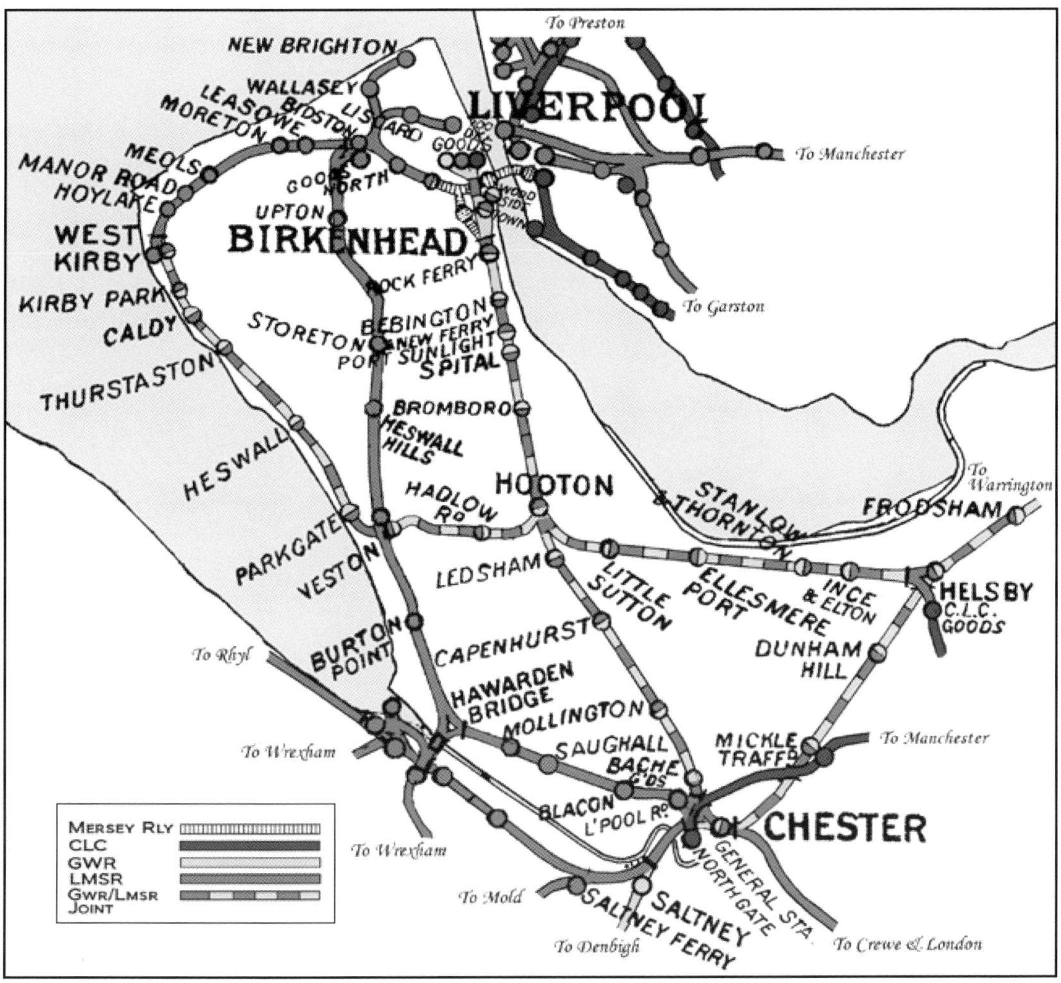

GEOGRAPHICAL SETTING

The Wirral peninsular is bounded on the east by the estuary of the River Mersey, on the west by that of the River Dee and on the north by that area of the Irish Sea known as Liverpool Bay. The district had been the Hundred of Wirral and was thinly populated.

Industrialisation began in 1824, when John Baird established an ironworks at Birkenhead. His famous shipbuilding yard followed, as did other industries. Wirral is fairly flat on its east side, but there are hills rising to 270ft on its west flank. The area is formed of various sandstones and was in the county of Cheshire when the railways were built.

The maps are to the scale of 25ins to 1 mile, with north at the top, unless otherwise indicated.

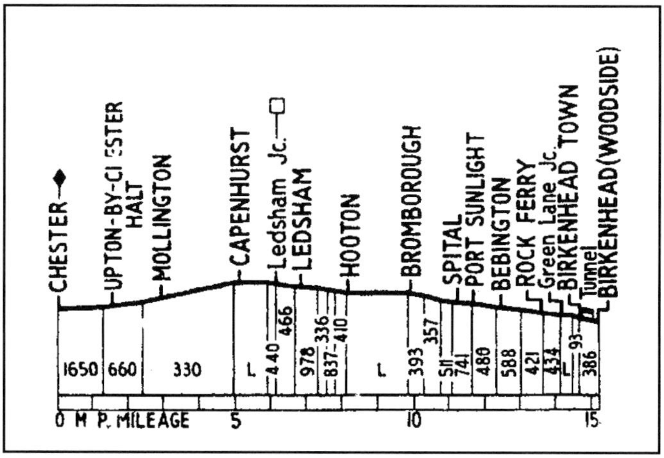

Gradient profile, showing the names in use in 1940.

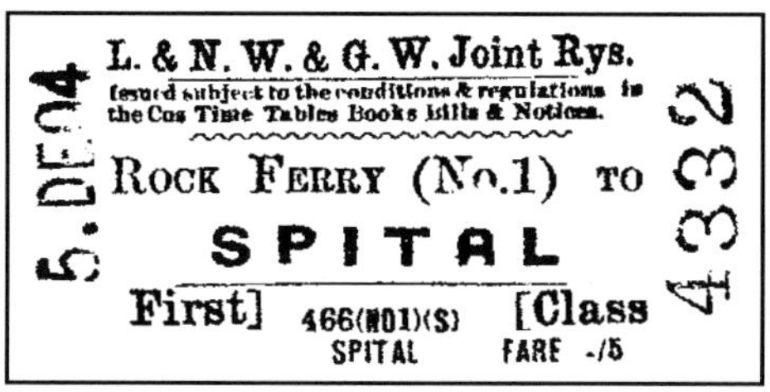

HOOTON and HELSBY.—Birkenhead.—London and North Western and Great Western.

Miles	Up.	Week Days.															Weds. and Sats.	Sn
		mrn	mrn	mrn	mrn	mrn	aft	aft	aft	aft	aft	aft	aft	aft	aft	aft	aft	mrn
	472 Chester (General Sta.)..dep	....	7 25	8 45	1012	1140	1245	1 e 5	1 s 5	2 40	3e52	5 0	6 5	7 38	9 8	....	1120	....
	473 Birkenhead (Woodside) "	6 30	7 45	8 45	1020	1125	1245	1 e 0	1s25	2 45	3e55	5 12	6 5	7 35	9 0	10 u 0	1120	....
—	Hooton .....dep.	7 0	8 25	9 10	1037	12 0	1 10	1e30	1s45	3 20	4e15	5 34	6 27	8 6	9 27	10u30	1155	6 20
1¾	Little Sutton	7 5	8 30	9 15	1042	12 5	1 15	1e35	1s50	3 25	4e20	5 39	6 32	8 11	9 32	10u35	12 0	....
3¾	Ellesmere Port.....	7 9	8 34	9 19	1046	12 9	1 20	1e39	1s54	3 29	4e24	5 43	6 36	8 15	9 37	10u40	12 5	6 29
7	Ince and Elton.....	7 18	8 41	9 26	1053	1216	....	1e46	2 s 1	3 36	4e31	5 51	6 43	8 22	....	....	....	6 35
9	Helsby 474, 484, 485 .....arr.	7 23	8 45	9 30	1057	1220	....	1e50	2 s 5	3 40	4e35	5 55	6 47	8 26	....	....	....	6 45

Miles	Down.	Week Days.								Except Sats.					Sn
		mrn	mrn	mrn	mrn	aft	aft	aft	aft	aft	aft	aft	aft	aft	mrn
	Helsby .....dep	7 55	9 0	10 0	1115	1230	....	2 35	4 0	5 20	6 9	7 10	8 45	....	7 10
2	Ince and Elton.....	8 1	9 5	10 5	1121	1236	....	2 41	4 8	5 26	6 15	7 16	8 51	....	7 15
5½	Ellesmere Port.....	8 6	9 9	10 9	1126	1241	1 50	2 46	4 13	5 30	6 20	7 21	8 56	1010	7 21
7¼	Little Sutton	8 12	9 14	1015	1132	1247	1 55	2 52	4 19	5 36	6 26	7 27	9 2	1015	....
9	Hooton 471, 472, 473.....arr.	8 16	9 18	1019	1136	1251	2 0	2 56	4 23	5 40	6 30	7 31	9 6	1020	7 32
15½	472 Birkenhead (Woodside) arr.	8 36	9 35	1045	12 5	1 21	2 26	3 26	4 47	6 17	6 56	8 0	9 39	1049	1021
17	473 Chester (General Sta.).. "	8 53	9 33	1056	12 5	1 21	2 48	4 5	4 53	5 58	7 25	8 30	9 40	1048	9 29

e Except Saturdays. *s* Saturdays only. *u* Mondays, Tuesdays, and Fridays.

March 1909

HISTORICAL BACKGROUND

The Grand Junction Railway opened to Chester from Crewe on 1st October 1840, but the Chester & Birkenhead Railway had come into use on 23rd September of that year. Its Act was dated 12th July 1837 and the line had double track from 1847.

The Shrewsbury & Chester Railway brought trains from Wrexham from 1846, the Chester & Holyhead Railway operated to Bangor from 1848 and the Birkenhead, Lancashire & Cheshire Junction Railway ran from Warrington to Chester from 1850. In 1874, the Cheshire Lines Committee brought trains to Chester from Mouldsworth and, in 1890, the associated Manchester, Sheffield & Lincolnshire Railway ran trains from Chester westwards. This route became part of the Great Central Railway in 1897, but closed to passengers in 1968. The line north from it to Bidston was opened by the North Wales & Liverpool Railway in 1896; it was under GCR control from 1905 and remains in use today for trains from Wrexham.

After two name changes, the C&BR became the Joint Line of the Great Western and the London & North Western Railways in 1860. The line between Helsby and Hooton was their Joint venture and it opened on 1st July 1863. There was a link from the former to Mouldsworth from 1869 until 1991, from a junction just west of Helsby.

The north end of the Wirral area was served by another Joint Line from Hooton, to West Kirby. This place had been linked in 1878 to Hoylake, which had been served by the Hoylake Railway from Birkenhead since 1866. It underwent two name changes and became the Wirral Railway in 1891. It linked up with the Mersey Railway at Birkenhead Park in 1888. In 1886, this company had begun running trains through the Mersey Tunnel and on to a terminus at St. James Street, Liverpool. It was extended to Central station in 1892. The MR had tunnelled under Birkenhead to Green Park, where it met the Joint Line from Chester.

Quadrupling took place between Ledsham and Green Lane in 1902-08 and is detailed in the pictures.

The grouping in 1923 resulted in the LNWR becoming part of the London Midland & Scottish Railway, but the GWR retained its identity. The GCR became a constituent of the London & North Eastern Railway. The Wirral Railway went into the LMS, but the Mersey Railway remained independent until nationalisation in 1948. The LMS then formed most of the London Midland Region of British Railways, the LNER the Eastern Region and the GWR the Western Region. The Joint Lines to Birkenhead remained joint until 1951, when they became the responsibility of the LMR. The CLC and the Mersey Railway were LMR from 1948.

The route between Shotton and West Kirby closed to passengers on 17th September 1956; goods closures are given in the captions. The routes included in this album remain in use and privatisation resulted in Merseyrail Electrics Ltd having a 7 year 2 month franchise from 19th January 1997. It excluded the line east of Ellesmere Port, which went to North Western Trains Ltd. Arriva Trains Merseyside operated the former from February 2000 and Merseyrail took over on 20th July 2003. The Helsby routes later became part of Northern Rail.

Electrification

Liverpool Central to Rock Ferry and Birkenhead Park was operated from 3rd May 1903 by DC current at 750 volts, using conductor rails. It eliminated the appalling effect of steam haulage in tunnels graded at mostly 1 in 27.

There was a long interval before the electrification was extended. It reached Hooton on 30th September 1985, Chester on 7th October 1993 and Ellesmere Port on 29th May 1994.

PASSENGER SERVICES

The tables below show the total number of down trains running on at least five days per week.

Chester to Birkenhead

	Weekdays	Sundays
1840	5	2
1863	13	5
1885	22	6
1909	36	10

A good frequency of fast and stopping trains lasted into the 1960s. From March to November 1967, Birkenhead Woodside received only a DMU hourly from Chester, after which time the service was cut back to Rock Ferry and a change was needed to electric trains running from there to Liverpool. The extension of electric services south to Hooton brought a basic four trains per hour service from 1985, with connections twice an hour to Chester and once to Helsby. The Sunday figures were 2, 1 and 0. Chester-Helsby trains ran through, reversing at Hooton.

Electrification in 1993 to Chester provided the same time intervals, but an erratic service on the Helsby Line for seven months. Thereafter, Ellesmere Port had two per hour westwards and one eastwards, but none on Sundays on the Helsby side.

Hooton to Helsby

	Weekdays	Sundays
1869	6	0
1885	6	0
1909	11	1
1932	17	4
1955	17	5
1968	13	0

The service west of Ellesmere Port was enhanced in the 1930s and 1940s, in particular. The provisions after 1985 are described in the paragraphs above.

Table 192 CHESTER and BIRKENHEAD

Week Days

Miles		a.m	a.m	a.m		a.m	a.m	a.m	a.m	a.m	a.m	a.m	a.m	a.m	a.m	a.m		a.m	a.m	a.m		a.m	a.m
—	Chester .... dep	..	..	6 23	..	..	6 57	..	7 45	..	8 15	..	..	8 23	8 42	..	..	..	9 2	..	..	9 27	..
1½	Upton-by-Chester Halt..	..	..	..	..	..	7 1	..	7 48	..	..	..	..	8 26	..	..	..	..	9 5	..	..	..	..
3	Mollington..............	..	..	..	..	..	7 6	..	7 53	..	..	..	..	8 30	..	..	..	..	9 9	..	..	..	..
5	Capenhurst..............	..	..	6 37	..	..	7 12	..	7 59	..	..	..	..	8 35	..	..	..	..	9 14	..	..	..	..
6¼	Ledsham	..	..	..	..	..	7 18	..	8 4	..	..	..	..	8 4[illegible]	..	..	..	..	9 19	..	..	..	..
8	Hooton..................	6 39	6 51	6‡52	..	7 8	7 28	7 55	8 12	8 14	..	8 25	8 40	8 47	..	9 5	..	9 10	..	9 28	..	9 41	9 40
9½	Bromborough...........	..	..	6 56	..	7 11	7 32	7 58	8 16	8 18	..	8 28	8 43	8 50	..	..	..	9 13	..	9 21	..	..	9 43
11	Spital	6 44	..	7 1	..	7 15	7 37	..	8 21	..	..	8 32	..	8 54	..	..	..	9 17	..	9 35	..	..	9 47
11½	Port Sunlight	6 46	..	7 4	..	7 17	7 41	8 3	8 24	..	8 35	..	..	8 56	..	..	..	9 19	..	..	..	..	9 49
12¼	Bebington & New Ferry.	6 49	..	7 8	..	7 20	7 45	..	8 29	8 24	..	..	8 49	8 59	..	..	..	9 22	..	9 40	..	..	9 52
13¼	Rock Ferry......... arr	6 52	7 0	7 11	..	7 23	7 49	8 8	8 32	8 27	8 41	8 39	8 52	9 2	9 1	9 14	..	9 27	9 30	9 43	..	9 49	9 57
15¼	Birkenhead (W.).... "	7 0	7 9	7 19	..	7 34	7 58	8 16	8 40	8 35	8 48	8 54	..	9 12	9 8	9 22	..	9 33	9 40	..	..	9 57	10 4

Week Days—continued

	a.m	a.m	a.m		a.m	a.m		p.m	p.m		p.m		p.m		p.m	p.m	p.m		p.m	p.m		p.m	p.m
			A			E		S			S				S	A						S	S
Chester .... dep	10 7	..	..	..	11 5	..	..	..	12 5	..	..	..	1232	..	..	..	1 30	..	..	2 34	..	..	..
Upton-by-Chester Halt..	..	..	..	..	..	..	..	..	12 8	..	..	..	1235	..	..	..	..	..	..	..	..	..	..
Mollington..............	..	..	..	..	..	..	..	..	1212	..	..	..	1239	..	..	..	..	..	..	..	..	..	..
Capenhurst..............	..	..	..	..	..	..	..	..	1218	..	..	..	1244	..	..	..	..	..	..	..	..	..	..
Ledsham	..	..	..	..	..	..	..	..	..	..	..	..	1249	..	..	..	..	..	..	..	..	..	..
Hooton..................	1022	1028	11 0	..	1120	1153	..	1215	1229	..	1235	..	1255	..	1 4	1 42	1 47	..	2 37	2 49	..	3 22	3 25
Bromborough...........	..	1031	11 3	..	..	1156	..	1218	..	..	1240	..	1258	..	1 7	1 45	1 50	..	2 40	..	..	3 25	..
Spital	..	1035	11 7	..	..	12 0	..	1222	..	..	1244	..	1 2	..	1 11	1 49	1 54	..	2 44	..	..	3 29	..
Port Sunlight	..	1037	11 9	..	..	12 5	..	1227	..	..	1249	..	1 4	..	1 14	1 51	1 56	..	2 47	..	..	3 32	..
Bebington & New Ferry.	..	1040	1112	..	..	12 8	..	1230	..	..	1252	..	1 10	..	1 17	1 54	1 59	..	2 50	..	..	3 35	..
Rock Ferry......... arr	1030	1043	1115	..	1128	1211	..	1234	1237	..	1256	..	1 13	..	1 21	1 57	2 2	..	2 53	2 57	..	3 38	3 33
Birkenhead (W.).... "	1038	1051	..	..	1136	1219	..	1241	1245	..	1 4	..	1 21	..	1 29	..	2 10	..	3 1	3 5	..	3 46	3 41

Week Days—continued

	p.m	p.m		p.m	p.m		p.m	p.m		p.m	p.m	p.m		p.m	p.m	p.m		p.m	p.m	p.m	p.m		p.m
		E		E			S	E		S	E					E		S	E				
Chester .... dep	3 16	..	..	..	4 18	..	4 30	4 30	..	..	..	5 10	..	5 39	..	5 55	..	5 55	..	..	6 20	..	..
Upton-by-Chester Halt..	..	..	..	..	..	..	4 33	4 33	..	..	..	5 13	..	..	..	5 58	..	5 58	..	..	6 23	..	..
Mollington..............	..	..	..	..	..	..	4 37	4 37	..	..	..	5 17	..	..	..	6 2	..	6 2	..	..	6 27	..	..
Capenhurst..............	..	..	..	..	..	..	4 42	4 42	..	..	..	5 23	..	5 47	..	6 7	..	6 7	..	..	6 32	..	..
Ledsham	..	..	..	..	..	..	4 47	4 47	..	..	..	5 28	..	..	..	..	..	..	..	..	6 37	..	..
Hooton..................	3 38	4 15	..	4 23	4 33	..	4 54	5 1	..	5 8	5 21	5 34	..	5 55	5 55	6 16	..	6 16	6 25	6 34	6 45	..	6 58
Bromborough...........	..	4 18	..	4 26	..	..	4 57	5 4	..	5 11	5 25	..	..	..	5 59	6 19	..	6 19	6 28	6 37	..	..	7 2
Spital	..	4 22	..	4 30	..	..	5 1	5 8	..	5 15	5 30	..	..	..	6 4	..	..	6 23	6 32	..	..	..	7 7
Port Sunlight	..	4 25	..	4 33	..	..	5 4	5 11	..	5 19	5 37	5 44	..	..	6 9	..	..	6 25	6 34	6 42	..	..	7 10
Bebington & New Ferry.	..	4 28	..	4 36	..	..	5 7	5 15	..	5 23	5 41	..	..	..	6 13	..	..	6 28	6 37	..	..	..	7 14
Rock Ferry......... arr	3 47	4 31	..	4 39	4 42	..	5 10	5 18	..	5 27	5 46	5 51	..	6 8	6 16	6 27	..	6 32	6 41	6 47	6 53	..	7 18
Birkenhead (W.).... "	3 52	4 39	..	4 47	4 50	..	5 18	5 26	..	5 37	5 51	5 58	..	6 11	6 24	6 35	..	6 41	6 50	..	7 1	..	7 26

May 1948

CHESTER, HOOTON, BIRKENHEAD, and LIVERPOOL.—Birkenhead—L. & N. W. and G. W.

Miles	Down.	aft	mrn (Except Mondays.)	mrn	mrn	mrn	mrn	mrn	mrn	mrn	mrn	mrn	mrn	mrn (From Heswall at 9 15 mrn., see p. 471.)	mrn	n (From Ruabon at 9 3 mrn., see p. 71.)	mrn	mrn	mrn	mrn	mrn	mrn
	Exchange Station, 484 MANCHESTER ....dep.	1125	o	...	...	...	...	6 45	...	...	7 40	...	7 40		...		8 5	...	...	...	...	...
	Chester (General Sta.)..dep.	2 50	6 30	7 25	...	...	8 10	8 40	...	8 45	9 6	...	9 15		9 20		9 50	...	...	1012	1020	1045
3	Mollington	...		7 34	...	...	8 17	...	...	...	...	...	9 21		...		...	...	...	...	1027	...
5	Capenhurst	...		7 41	...	...	8 23	...	...	8 54	...	...	...		9 29		...	...	...	...	1033	...
6¾	Ledsham	...		7 47	...	...	8 28	...	...	8 58	...	...	...		9 34		...	...	...	1024	1038	...
8	Hooton 470, 471	...		7 55	8 17	8 21	8 32	...	9 0	9 2	...	9 19	...		9 39		...	1012	1015	1028	1043	...
9½	Bromborough	...		8 0	8 22	...	8 37	...	...	9 7	...	...	...		9 44		...	...	1020	...	1048	...
11	Spital	...		8 4	8 26	...	8 41	8 54	...	9 11	...	...	9 32		9 48		...	...	1024	...	1052	...
12¼	Bebington and New Ferry	...		8 8	8 30	...	8 45	...	...	9 15	...	...	...		9 52		...	...	1028	...	1056	...
13¼	Rock Ferry	...	g	8 10	8 32	8 29	8 47	9 0	9 10	9 17	9 24	9 27	9 36	9 40	9 54	9 59	10 9	1020	1030	1035	1058	11 3
15⅝	Liverpool (James St.) arr.	...	7 0	8 22	8 47	8 41	9 0	9 12	9 25	9 31	9 37	9 37	9 50	9 50	10 9	10 9	1022	1034	1041	1047	1112	1118
16¼	" (Cen. L. L.) "	...	7 2	8 24	8 49	8 43	9 2	9 14	9 27	9 33	9 39	9 39	9 52	9 52	1011	1011	1024	1036	1043	1049	1114	1120
	Birkenhead { Town	...	...	8 18	g	...	g	...	...	g	...	g	...	...	10 0	...	...	...	g	g	g	...
14½	Birkenhead { Woodside	3 15	6 56	8 23	8 40	8 36	8 55	9 7	9 16	9 27	9 31	9 35	9 44	9 47	10 3	10 7	1016	1026	1040	1045	11 6	1111
15	Liverpool * 479, 772 ..arr.	3 40	7 10	8 40	9 0	8 50	9 10	9 20	9 30	9 40	9 50	9 50	10 0	10 0	1020	1020	1030	1040	11 0	11 0	1120	1130

Week Days—Continued.

Down.	mrn	n (From Shrewsbury at 10 5 mn., see p. 71.)	mrn	mrn	non	aft	mrn	aft	aft	aft	aft	aft (Sats. only.)	aft	aft	aft	aft	aft	aft	aft	aft	aft	aft
Exchange Station, 484 MANCHESTER ....dep.	9 45		...	...	...	...	1045	...	b	1225	s		1 5	...	...	...	...	...	2 40	...	...	3 40
Chester (General Sta.)..dep.	1110		...	1140	...	...	1245	1 5	1 18	1 55	...		2 40	...	3 45	3 52	3 55	...	4 25	4 35	...	5 0
Mollington	...		...	...	...	...	...	1 12	...	...	...		2 47	...	...	...	4 2	...	b	...	...	...
Capenhurst	...		...	...	...	...	1253	1 18	...	...	...		2 53	...	...	...	4 8	...	b	...	...	...
Ledsham	...		...	1152	...	...	...	1 23	...	...	...		2 58	...	...	...	4 13	...	b	...	...	...
Hooton 470, 471	...		1150	1156	12 0	1248	1 2	1 28	...	2 10	2 16	2 54	3 3	3 38	3 58	4 5	4 16	4 24	b	...	4 50	5 14
Bromborough	...		...	...	12 5	1253	...	1 33	...	...	2 21	...	3 8	3 43	...	4 10	...	4 29	b	...	4 55	...
Spital	...		...	...	12 9	...	...	1 37	...	...	2 25	...	3 12	3 47	...	...	...	4 33	b	...	4 59	...
Bebington and New Ferry	...		...	...	1213	h	...	1 41	...	...	2 29	...	3 16	3 51	...	...	...	4 37	b	...	5 3	...
Rock Ferry	1128	1143	1158	12 4	1215	1259	1 11	1 43	1 37	2 18	2 31	3 2	3 18	3 53	4 6	4 17	...	4 39	4 46	4 52	5 5	5 23
Liverpool (James St.) arr.	1144	1156	12 9	1215	1228	1 12	1 25	1 56	1 50	2 28	2 41	3 12	3 31	4 3	4 22	4 28	...	4 53	5 0	5 6	5 18	5 37
" (Cen. L. L.) "	1146	1158	1211	1217	1230	1 14	1 27	1 58	1 52	2 30	2 43	3 14	3 33	4 5	4 24	4 30	...	4 55	5 2	5 8	5 20	5 39
Birkenhead { Town	...	...	...	...	g	g	g	g	...	...	g	...	3 23	g	...	g	...	g	g	g	g	g
Birkenhead { Woodside	1136	1150	12 5	1211	1224	1 7	1 21	1 51	1 45	2 26	2 39	3 9	3 26	4 1	4 16	4 27	...	4 47	4 55	5 0	5 15	5 32
Liverpool * 479, 772 ..arr.	1150	1210	1220	1230	1240	1 20	1 40	2 10	2 0	2 40	3 0	3 30	3 40	4 20	4 30	4 40	...	5 0	5 10	5 20	5 30	5 50

Week Days—Continued.

Down.	aft	aft	aft	aft	aft	aft	Through Carriage, L. & S. W. Line to Birkenhead (Woodside), see page 73.	aft	aft	aft	aft	Through Carriage, Dover, &c., to Birkenhead (Wdside) see p. 73	aft	aft	aft	n p	aft	aft	aft	aft	aft	
Exchange Station, 484 MANCHESTER ....dep.	...	...	4 55	...	...	...		5 10	...	...	...		7 15	...	...	...	...	...	...	...	9 30	...
Chester (General Sta.)..dep.	...	5 30	6 5	...	6 30	...		7 15	...	7 38	8 5		8 40	8 50	9 8	...		...	1030	1040	1120	...
Mollington	...	5 37	...	...	6 38	...		...	...	7 45	...		...	8 57	...	f	...	...	1037	...	1127	...
Capenhurst	...	5 43	...	...	6 45	...		...	...	7 51	...		...	9 3	...	f	...	...	1043	...	g	...
Ledsham	...	5 48	...	...	6 50	...		...	...	7 56	...		...	9 8	...	f	...	...	1048	...	1135	...
Hooton 470, 471	5 15	5 53	6 20	6 35	6 56	7 6		...	7 35	8 1	...		...	9 13	9 22	f	9 50	1026	1052	...	1139	...
Bromborough	5 20	5 58	6 25	6 40	7 1	...		...	7 40	8 6	...		...	9 18	...	f	9 55	1031	1057	...	a	...
Spital	...	6 2	6 29	6 44	7 5	...		...	7 44	8 10	...		...	9 22	...	f	9 59	1035	11 1	...	1145	...
Bebington and New Ferry	...	6 6	6 33	...	7 9	...		...	7 48	8 14	...		...	9 26	...	f	10 3	1039	11 5	...	g	...
Rock Ferry	5 26	6 8	6 35	6 48	7 11	715		7 37	7 50	8 16	8 25		9 4	9 28	9 36	9 59	10 5	1041	11 7	11 1	1152	...
Liverpool (James St.) arr.	5 37	6 22	6 47	7 0	7 25	731		7 50	8 3	8 28	8 41		9 18	9 44	9 50	10 9	1015	1053	1118	1112	12 6	...
" (Cen. L. L.) "	5 39	6 24	6 49	7 2	7 27	733		7 52	8 5	8 30	8 43		9 20	9 46	9 52	1011	1017	1055	1120	1114	12 8	...
Birkenhead { Town	g	g	6 42	6 53	g	...		...	g	g	8 32		g	g	g	...	...	...	...	...	...	...
Birkenhead { Woodside	5 36	6 17	6 45	6 56	7 20	724		r 46	8 0	8 27	8 35		9 15	9 39	9 45	10 6	1012	1049	1115	1110	12 0	...
Liverpool * 479, 772 ..arr.	5 50	6 30	7 0	7 10	7 40	740		8 0	8 20	8 40	8 50		9 30	10 0	10 0	1020	1030	1110	1140	1125	1220	...

Sundays.

Down.	Sat.	mrn	mrn	mrn	mrn	mrn	aft	aft	aft	aft	aft	aft			
Exchange Station, 484 MANCHESTER ....dep.	1125	b	7 50	...	...	...	...	...	...	...	6 0	...	...	...	...
Chester (General Sta.)..dep.	2 50	6 30	9 35	...	9 45	1125	2 10	4 35	5 45	7 0	8 40	10 5	...	...	...
Mollington	Sun	...	...	...	9 54	1133	2 17	4 42	5 52	7 8	8 47	1012	...	...	...
Capenhurst	mrn	...	...	...	10 0	1139	2 23	4 48	5 58	7 14	8 53	1018	...	...	...
Ledsham	...	...	...	...	10 5	1144	2 28	4 53	6 3	7 20	8 58	1023	...	...	...
Hooton 470, 471	...	k	...	10 6	1010	1149	2 33	4 58	6 8	7 25	9 3	1028	...	...	...
Bromborough	...	...	...	...	1015	1154	2 38	5 3	6 13	7 30	9 8	1033	...	...	...
Spital	...	...	...	...	1019	1158	2 42	5 7	6 17	7 34	9 12	1037	...	...	...
Bebington and New Ferry	...	...	...	...	1023	12 2	2 46	5 11	6 21	7 38	9 16	1041	...	...	...
Rock Ferry	...	g	9 53	1014	1025	12 4	2 48	5 13	6 23	7 40	9 18	1043	...	...	...
Liverpool (James St.) arr.	...	...	10 3	1028	1041	1215	3 0	5 25	6 34	7 50	9 31	1053	...	...	...
" (Cen. L. L.) "	...	...	10 5	1030	1043	1217	3 2	5 27	6 36	7 52	9 33	1055	...	...	...
Birkenhead { Town	...	...	...	...	1032	g	g	g	6 32	7 52	g	...	...	...	...
Birkenhead { Woodside	3 15	6 56	10 0	1021	1035	1212	2 56	5 29	6 35	7 55	9 27	1053	...	...	...
Liverpool 479, 772 ..arr.	3 40	7 25	1020	1040	1050	1240	3 10	5 40	6 50	8 10	9 40	1110	...	...	...

☞ The Through Trains from Chester to Birkenhead (except the 2 50 mrn. daily and 6 30 mrn. Sundays) will stop at intermediate Stations to set down Passengers booked through from Bridgnorth, Stafford, Wolverhampton, Hereford, or Stations beyond, Cambrian Line, Ireland, or Scotland, on notice being given to the Guard at Chester.

a Stops to take up and also to set down Through Passengers.
b Stops to set down from London on informing the Guard at Chester.
b G. W. Tickets not available Manchester to Chester.
f Stops at any Station between Chester and Birkenhead to set down from Wolverhampton (G.W.) or beyond on informing Guard at Wrexham.
g Stop to set down on informing the Guard.
h Stops on Saturdays to take up for Birkenhead and Liverpool.
k Stops to set down from Wolverhampton, Hereford, or beyond, or from the Cambrian Line on informing Guard at Chester.
n L. & N. W. Tickets not available.
o Leaves at 10 35 aft. on Sundays.
p From London (Paddington) at 4 55 aft., see page 72.
r From Corwen at 7 35 mrn., see page 101.
s Saturdays only.
* Landing Stage.

March 1909

May 1948 continued

Week Days—continued

	p.m E		p.m S		p.m S		p.m		p.m		p.m		p.m		p.m		p.m		p.m		p.m	p.m	
Chester ....dep	7 0	..	7 0	..	..	..	7 24	..	..	..	..	..	8 40	..	9 27	..	..	..	1010	..	11 15	1142	..
Upton-by-Chester Halt..	..	..	7 3	..	..	..	..	..	..	..	..	..	8 43	..	..	..	..	..	1014	..	..	..	..
Mollington	..	..	7 7	..	..	..	..	..	..	..	..	..	8 47	..	..	..	..	..	1019	..	11S20	..	..
Capenhurst	..	..	7 12	..	..	..	..	..	..	..	..	..	8 52	..	..	..	..	..	1025	..	..	..	..
Ledsham	..	..	7 17	..	..	..	..	..	..	..	..	..	8 57	..	..	..	..	..	1031	..	11S30	..	..
Hooton	7 17	..	7 24	..	7 31	..	7 38	..	7 55	..	8 50	..	9 5	..	9 41	..	9 53	..	1040	..	11 35	1136	..
Bromborough	..	..	..	..	7 34	..	..	..	7 58	..	8 54	..	..	..	..	..	9 57	..	1044	..	11 39	..	..
Spital	..	..	..	..	7 38	..	..	..	8 2	..	8 59	..	..	..	..	..	10 2	..	1049	..	11 44	..	..
Port Sunlight	..	..	..	..	7 40	..	..	..	8 4	..	9 2	..	..	..	..	..	10 7	..	1052	..	..	..	..
Bebington & New Ferry	..	..	..	..	7 45	..	..	..	8 7	..	9 6	..	..	..	..	..	1011	..	1056	..	11 49	..	..
Rock Ferry ....arr	7 27	..	7 32	..	7 49	..	7 47	..	8 10	..	9 10	..	9 13	..	9 49	..	1017	..	11 0	..	11 53	12 6	..
Birkenhead (W.) .... "	7 33	..	7 40	..	7 59	..	7 54	..	8 20	..	9 17	..	9 22	..	9 57	..	1023	..	11 8	..	12 3	1216	..

Sundays

	a.m	a.m		a.m	a.m	a.m		p.m	p.m		p.m		p.m	p.m		p.m	p.m		p.m	p.m	p.m	p.m	
Chester ....dep	7 25	7 40	..	..	1020	1140	..	1230	..	..	4 25	..	6 0	..	..	7 55	8 42	..	9 10	10 5	..	11 5	..
Upton-by-Chester Halt..	..	..	..	..	1023	1143	..	..	..	..	4 28	..	6 4	..	..	..	8 46	..	..	..	..	..	..
Mollington	..	7 47	..	..	1027	1147	..	..	..	..	4 32	..	6 9	..	..	..	8 51	..	..	1011	..	..	..
Capenhurst	..	7 54	..	..	1032	1152	..	..	..	..	4 37	..	6 15	..	..	..	8 57	..	..	1017	..	..	..
Ledsham	..	..	..	..	1037	1157	..	..	..	..	..	..	6 20	..	..	..	9 2	..	..	1022	..	..	..
Hooton	7 40	8 5	..	9 58	1043	12 3	..	1244	2 38	..	4 48	..	6 27	6 41	..	8 12	9 9	..	9 24	1028	1038	1119	..
Bromborough	..	..	..	10 1	1046	12 6	..	..	2 41	..	4 51	..	6 31	6 45	..	8 15	9 13	..	..	1032	..	..	..
Spital	..	..	..	10 5	1050	1210	..	..	2 45	..	4 55	..	6 36	6 50	..	..	9 18	..	..	1037	..	..	..
Port Sunlight	..	..	..	10 7	1053	1213	..	..	2 47	..	4 58	..	..	..	..	..	9 21	..	..	..	..	..	..
Bebington & New Ferry	..	..	..	1010	1056	1216	..	..	2 50	..	5 1	..	6 41	6 57	..	..	9 24	..	..	1042	1044	..	..
Rock Ferry ....arr	7 48	8 13	..	1013	1059	1219	..	1252	2 53	..	5 4	..	6 45	7 1	..	8 23	9 27	..	9 32	1046	1047	1127	..
Birkenhead (W.) .... "	7 57	8 21	..	1021	11 7	1227	..	1 0	3 1	..	5 12	..	6 54	7 10	..	8 32	9 36	..	9 40	1054	1059	1135	..

E or E Except Saturdays. S or S Saturdays only. A Third class only ‡ Arr 6.44 a.m.

CHESTER

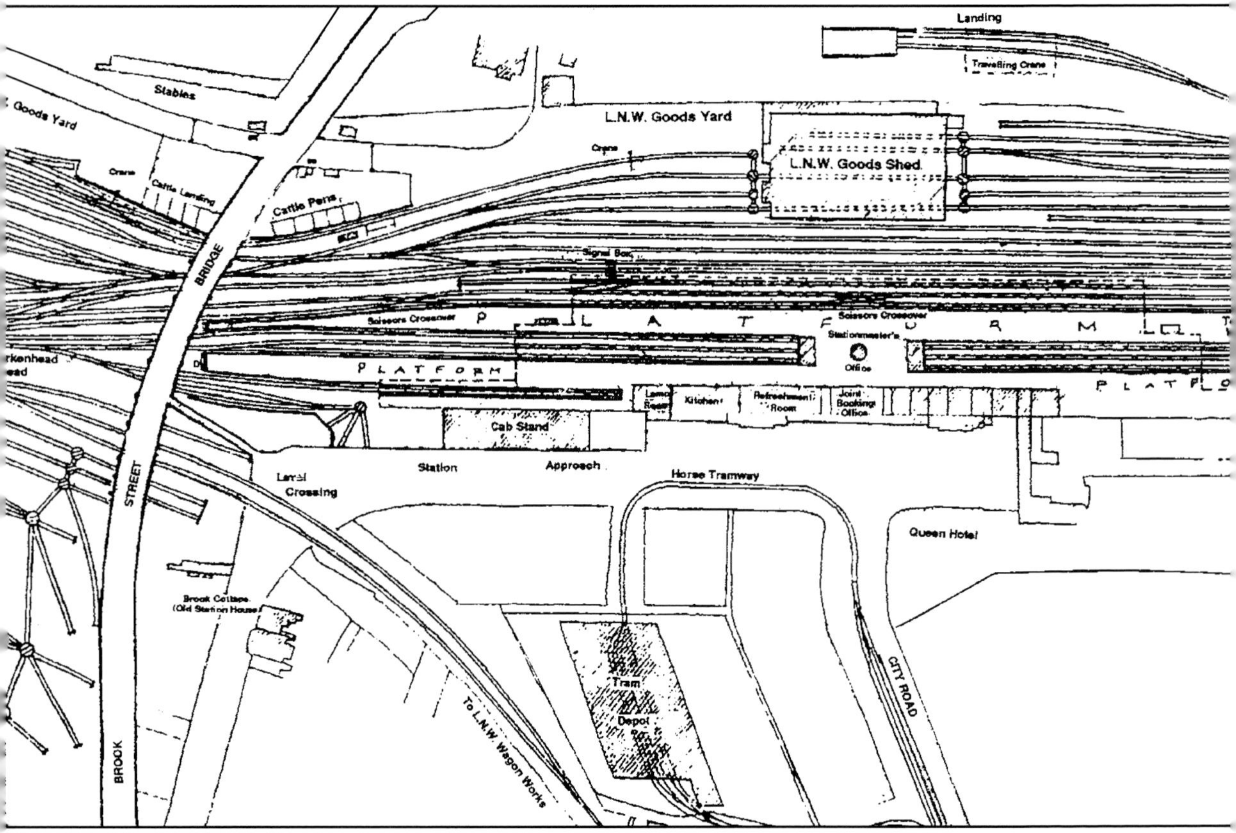

II. An 1884 official diagram indicates the arrangement before the enlargements, which began that year. There was only one through platform until that time.

1. A 1924 view west from the bridge running across both plans has the sidings in the foreground and No. 4 Box centre. The Birkenhead lines curve to the right beyond it. (Milepost 92½)

2. No. 2904 *Lady Godiva* stands with the 2.40pm Birkenhead to Paddington on 2nd June 1932. On the left is a "Fire Devil" which was lit on frosty nights to protect the water column. (H.C.Casserley)

III. The 1911 map at 15ins to 1 mile reveals the vast extent of the roof at its optimum. Tram tracks show, for full details see ***Chester Tramways (Middleton Press)***.

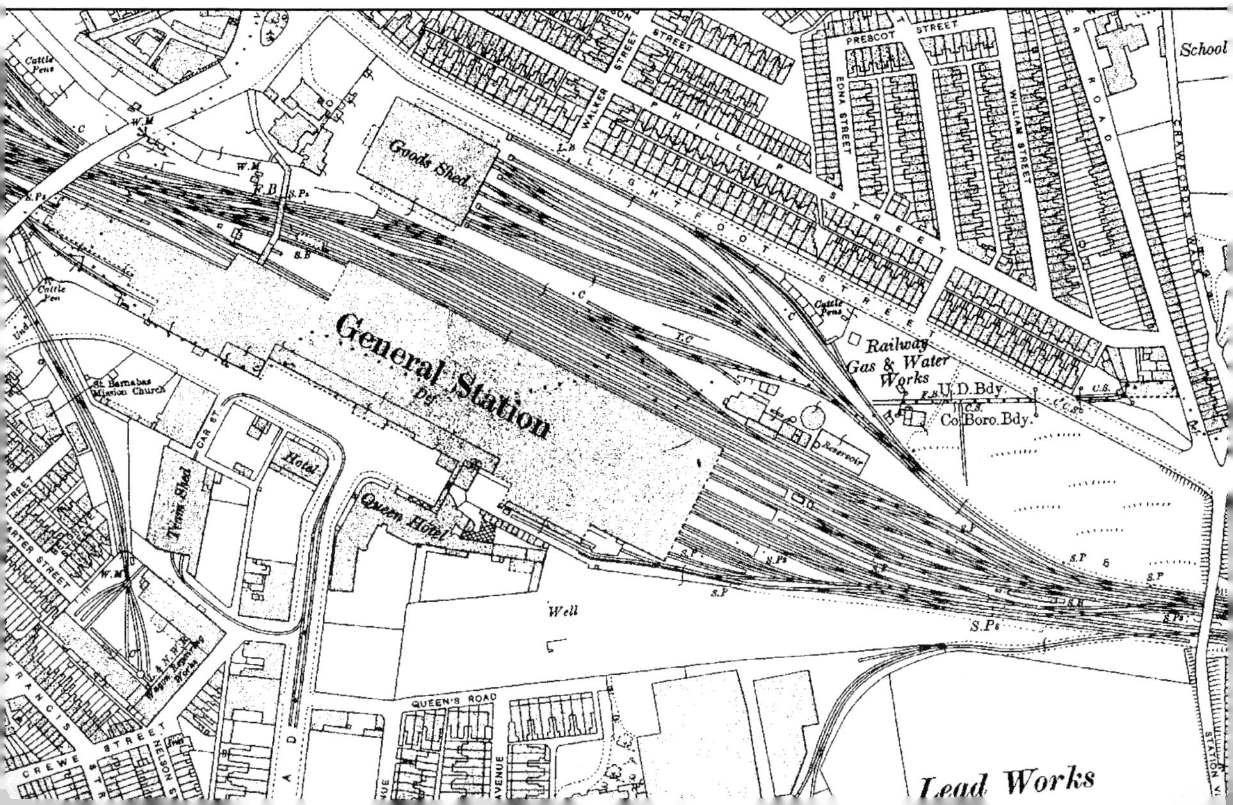

3. The roof appears to be still complete when photographed in about 1938, with a double headed train of unknown destination. (Milepost 92½)

IV. The 1903 Railway Clearing House diagram has had the signal box numbers added, together with their brief histories.

	Opened	Closed	No. of Levers
No. 1	01.1958	16.09.1973	60
No. 2	12.1890	06.05.1984	182
No. 3	07.1890	07.12.1980	45
No. 3A	09.1962	05.05.1984	85
No. 4	06.1904	06.05.1984	176
No. 5	05.1874	04.05.1984	81
No. 6	07.1903	05.05.1984	80

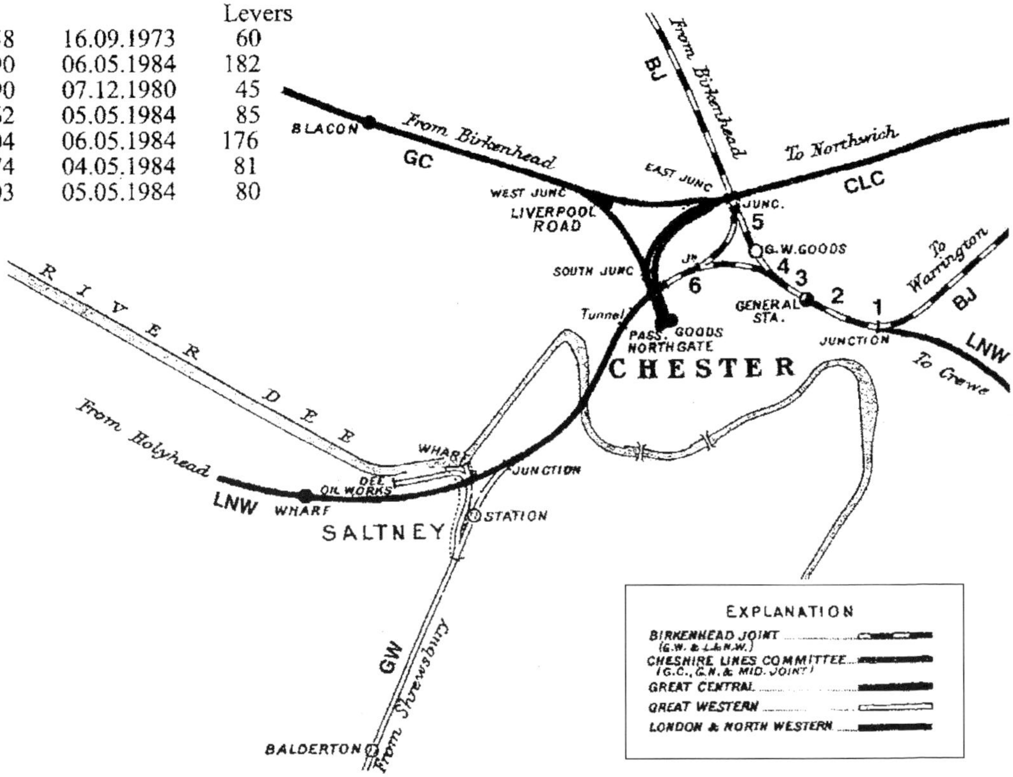

4. This is the north side of the station in about 1947 and an LMS 2-6-4T has arrived with a horsebox attached. The compartment coach suggests that it is a local train, possibly from Birkenhead. (Milepost 92½)

5. No. 4 Box is on the left and the engine sheds are on the right in this 1950s view. Centre are no. 6901 *Arley Hall* and no. 5970 *Hengrave Hall*. (A.W.V.Mace/Milepost 92½)

6. No. 42459 is waiting to leave for Birkenhead on 27th August 1964. Back in 1861, there was a staff of 279 of whom 138 were concerned with goods and 82 with passengers. (H.C.Casserley)

7. No. 4 Box is seen on the same day, together with its two main gantries. Trains for Holyhead and Shrewsbury turned left, the Birkenhead lines being both sides of the signal box. (H.C.Casserley)

Other views can be found in our *Chester to Rhyl* and *Shrewsbury to Chester* albums.

8. The up side was recorded on 21st June 1966, from the west end. The sign states GENERAL, a suffix used periodically. It was discontinued on 6th May 1970. The platforms were renumbered on 5th October 1980. (H.C.Casserley)

9. This view west on 7th August 1982 has the former LMS engine shed centre and the ex-GWR one on the right. This was fitted with a new roof in 1998, but demolished in 1999, due to privatisation fragmentation. (D.H.Mitchell)

10. No. 507026 is leaving for Liverpool at 12.25 on 22nd April 1994. There are conductor rails on both tracks in the foreground, but only one line behind the train is electrified, the one at platform 7. (T.Heavyside)

11. This is the 17.19 to Liverpool Central on 23rd April 1996. There was an alternative way to that city by DMU via Runcorn, avoiding submarine tunnels. (M.J.Stretton)

12. It is 23rd July 2001 and we can enjoy Francis Thompson's impressive frontage of 1848, one of the great railway stations of England. Some of this is occupied by non railway business, such as Hodges interiors, from the left as far as the canopy. Above the centre of the canopy is a large British Rail logo, where in an earlier era there was a sign "LMS & GW Railways". (A.C.Hartless)

13. The new shed was built for North Western Train's class 175 and 180 DMUs, but they were First North Western's by the time it was complete. Alston cared for the fleet. No. 507031 is working the 13.20 Chester to Liverpool on 2nd March 2002. The line on the right is a bypass for north-west and north-south freight trains and is known as Chester Curve. (P.Shannon)

BACHE

14. The station opened on 9th January 1984, replacing Upton-by-Chester, half a mile further north. There had been a goods station here earlier. The new site had a car park, a facility lacking at Upton; it was shared with the new Safeway supermarket. Passenger accommodation is meagre, but at least the place looks tidy. The train is the 15.05 Hooton to Chester, formed by class 101 nos 53325 and 53306 on 5th April 1986. (A.C.Hartless)

15. DMUs nos 51190 and 54353 are working the 15.01 Rock Ferry to Chester on 1st June 1984. The station was better situated to the new community than its predecessor. (H.Ballantyne)

UPTON-BY-CHESTER

16. The halt opened on 17th July 1939 and it is seen looking south in 1949. The suffix HALT was not used after 6th May 1968; the sign is of the LMS Hawkseye type. (Stations UK)

17. We look north in 1981 and see that steps were provided up to the road, which was the A5032 and then the A5116. As stated, closure came on 9th January 1984. Although the population had grown from 1769 in 1901 to 7708 in 1961, it was not close to the station. (Stations UK)

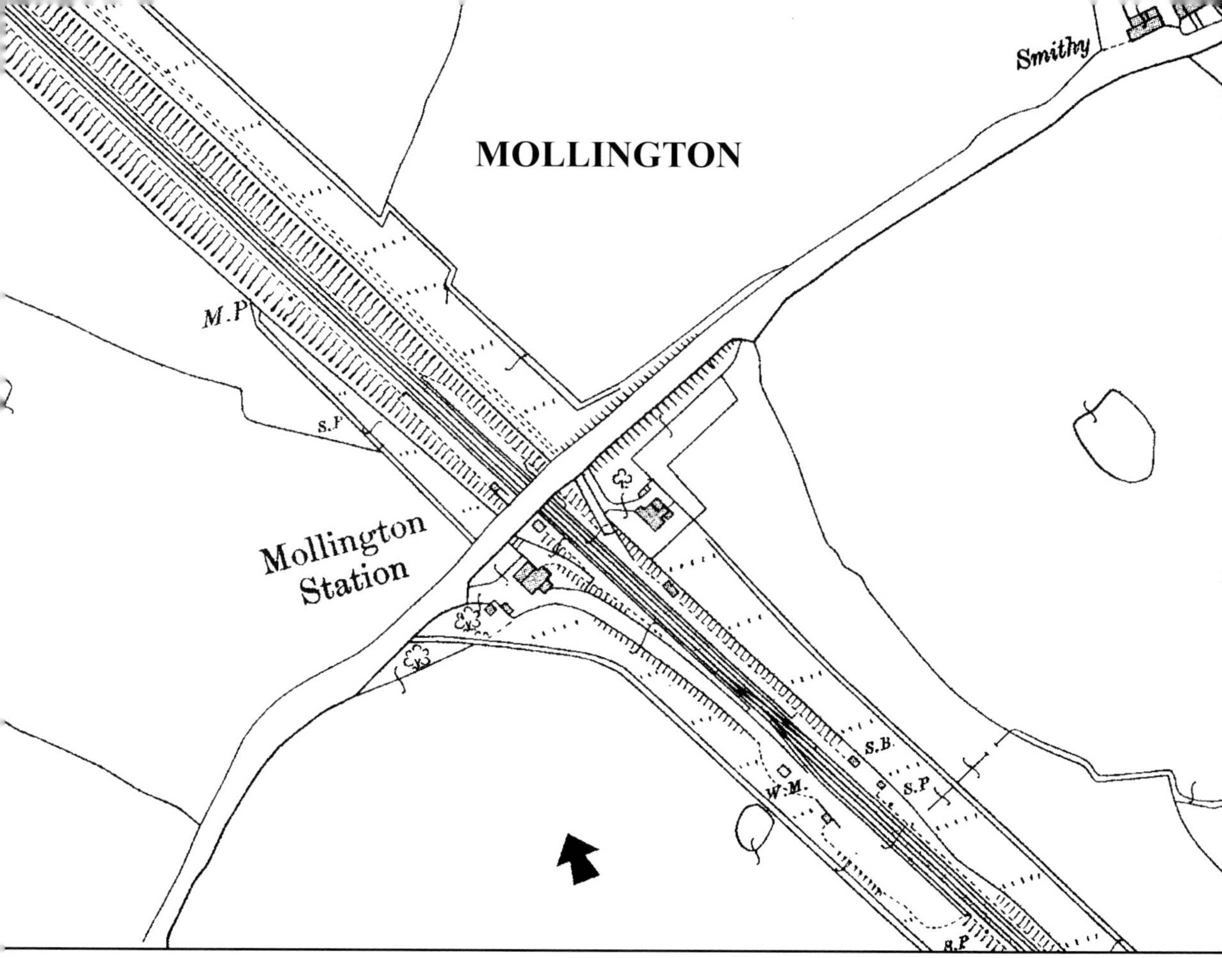

V. The 1911 map shows paths down to both platforms from the road, which never received a number, at least publicly. The village was ½ mile to the southwest and it housed only 182 folk in 1901.

Extract from Bradshaw's Guide for 1866. (Reprinted by Middleton Press 2011).

Chester to Birkenhead and Liverpool.

Leaving Chester, the first stations we pass are MOLLINGTON, LEDSHAM, and HOOTON, from the latter of which *Parkgate* is accessible by omnibus; the next place arrived at is

BROMBOROUGH, near to which is Eastham Ferry, the landing place for the Mersey steamers. It is a charming spot, and a place of great resort in the summer by pic-nic parties from Liverpool. Bromborough Mill, situated in a delightful dell.

SPITAL station.

BEBBINGTON.—Here is an old spire church, and just beyond are Upper Bebbington and the Stamton Stone Quarries, in which ripple marks have been found.

ROCK FERRY, between which and Liverpool steamers are constantly plying.

18. A 1951 view towards Birkenhead shows that both platforms continued under the bridge. The hut on the down one was the lamp room. The train will soon pass the 25-lever signal box, which replaced the one shown on the map. It opened on 6th October 1940 and served a new siding to an Air Ministry petrol depot. (Stations UK)

19. A panorama from the road bridge in 1960 includes the lane to the goods yard, which is lost in mist. Passenger traffic ceased on 7th March 1960, but the siding remained in use for wagon load traffic until 4th January 1965. The box was in the left distance and closed on 12th November 1980. (Stations UK)

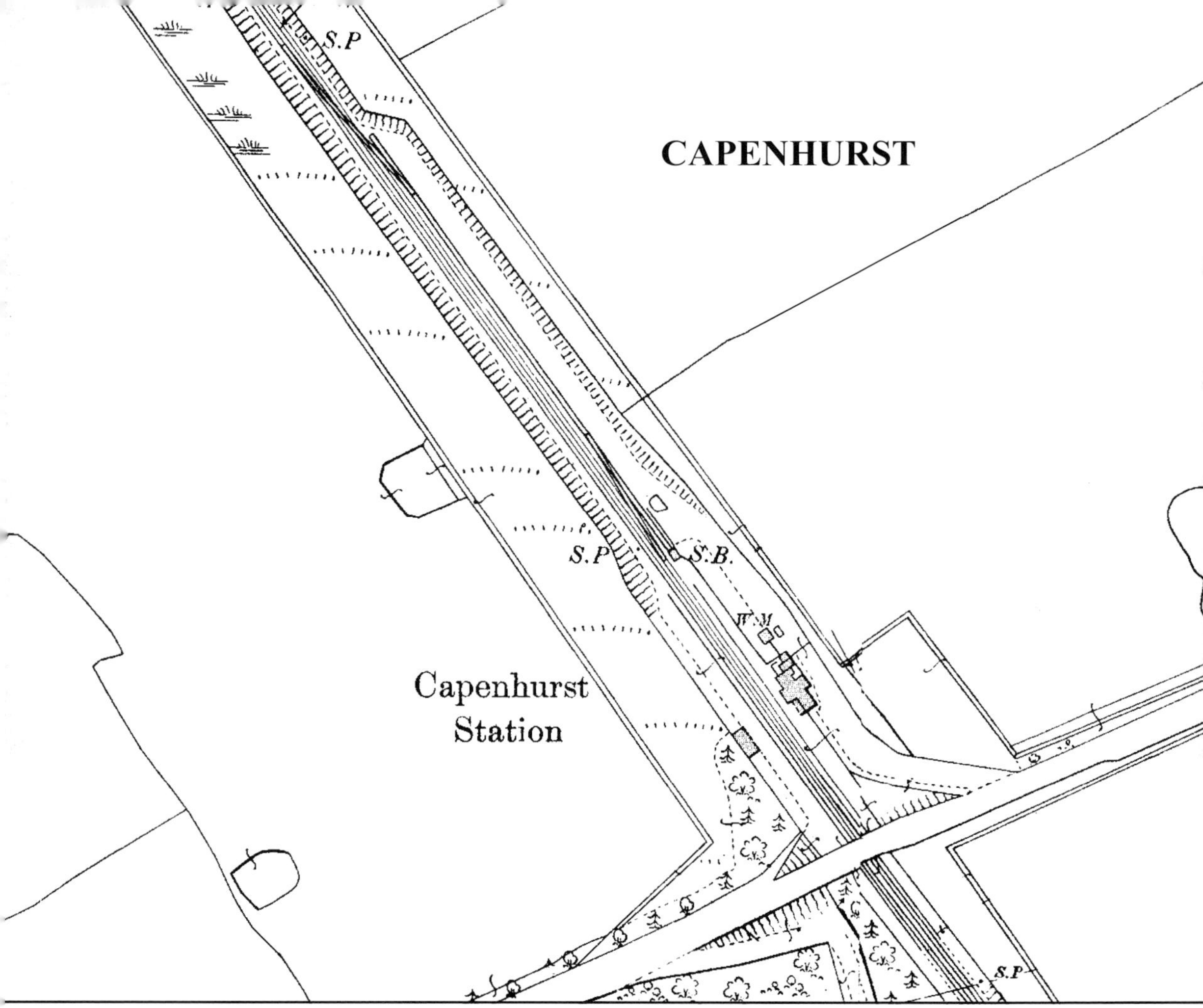

VI. The 1911 map shows a single loop in the goods yard. The station opened later than the route, on 1st August 1870.

20. A northward view in about 1930 includes an LNWR signal box, which lasted until 15th September 1940. It was replaced by a 65-lever flat-roofed one, which was needed for new sidings to a Royal Ordnance Factory. (Stations UK)

21. We look south on 2nd June 1961 and see the footbridge not marked on the 1901 map. The number of residents that year was 159. (R.M.Casserley)

22. A closer look at the main building on the same day includes early evidence of television. Staffing ceased here on 5th June 1972. (R.M.Casserley)

23. This 1960s view just excludes the signal box, which closed on 13th October 1968. The canopy glazing and shapely stanchions had gone, but the staff transport was well protected. (D.K.Jones coll.)

24. The down side was recorded on 11th June 1961, along with the starting signals. The small one was for the quadruple track, which started at Ledsham Junction. The goods yard closed on 5th April 1965. (H.C.Casserley)

25. No. 142027 arrives with the 12.31 Helsby to Chester on 23rd October 1991. Behind the high fence on the down side are the extensive premises of the Nuclear Decommissioning Agency, which began life as a WWII munitions factory. The switchgear on the opposite side of the tracks is part of the Urenco site, which produced enriched uranium for the nuclear industry. (A.C.Hartless)

26. This rearward view is of the same train, as in the last caption, departing for Chester. At least one passenger is present. The station building formerly occupied the ground at the extreme left. (A.C.Hartless)

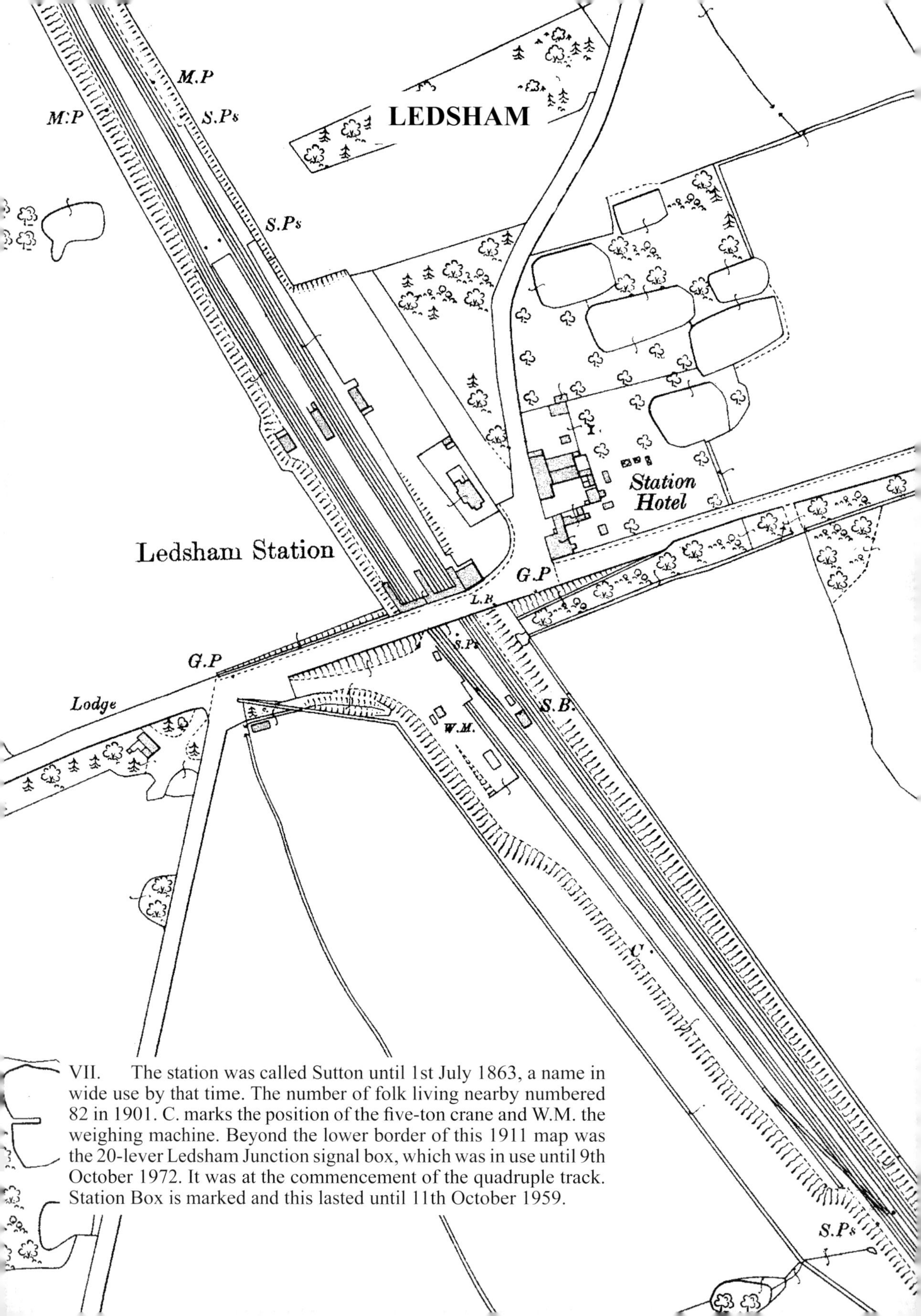

VII. The station was called Sutton until 1st July 1863, a name in wide use by that time. The number of folk living nearby numbered 82 in 1901. C. marks the position of the five-ton crane and W.M. the weighing machine. Beyond the lower border of this 1911 map was the 20-lever Ledsham Junction signal box, which was in use until 9th October 1972. It was at the commencement of the quadruple track. Station Box is marked and this lasted until 11th October 1959.

27. This northward view is from about 1930. This was the most southerly station on the quadruple track section, which was created in 1900-08. The station closed to both passenger and goods traffic on 20th July 1959. (Stations UK)

28. Looking in the other direction in 1947, we note the well protected footbridge and the up starting signals and distants. The line on the right was mainly used by goods trains and so the platform is probably being dismantled, rather than repaired. (Stations UK)

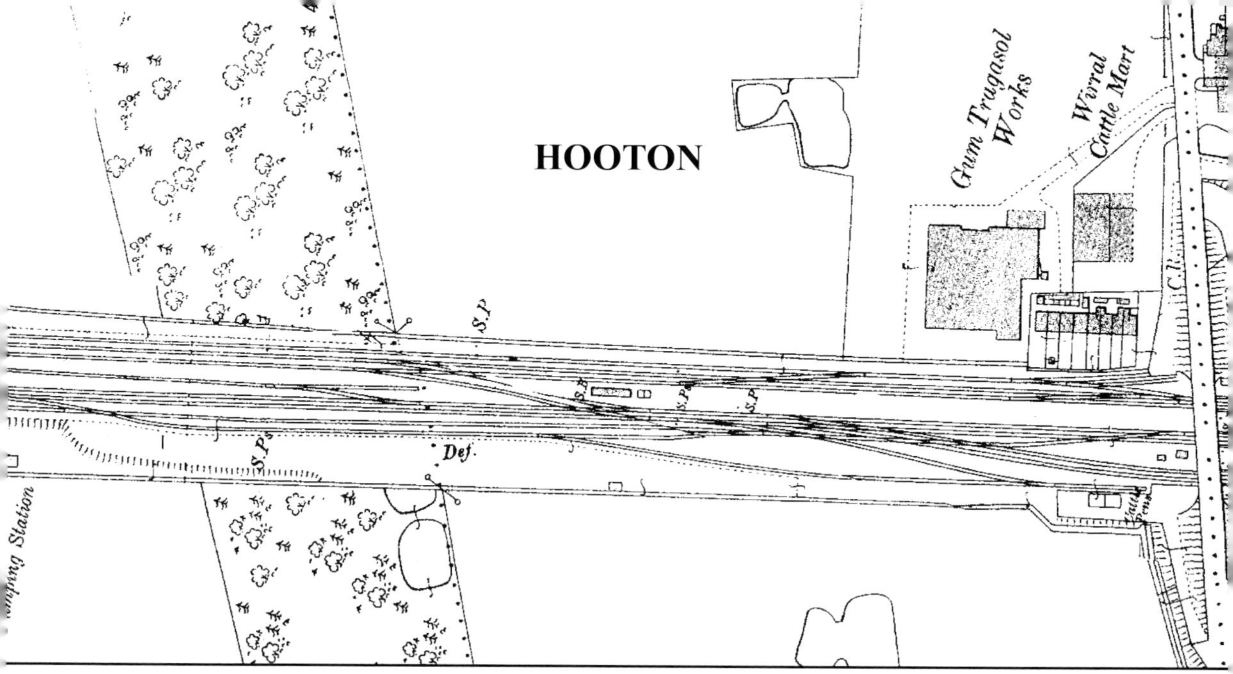

VIII. The 1912 edition has our route across both pages and the single line to West Kirby curving off the right one. The route to Ellesmere Port curves in the other direction, beyond the right border. The upper pair of tracks are the original ones. The station opened a few weeks after the line. On the left are sidings for cattle traffic and the waterworks. The population figures are surprising: 110 in 1851, 200 in 1901 and 537 in 2011. The village is more than ½ mile to the east.

29. This view north from South Junction box is from about 1910. It includes the goods shed, with the locomotive water tank alongside it. The ringed signals were for goods trains in LNWR days. The shed had been built for engines in 1848 and had one 0-4-2T in 1901, but closed in about 1925. To the right of it are the gates to a private siding, which runs behind the hedge to the waterworks. (Stations UK)

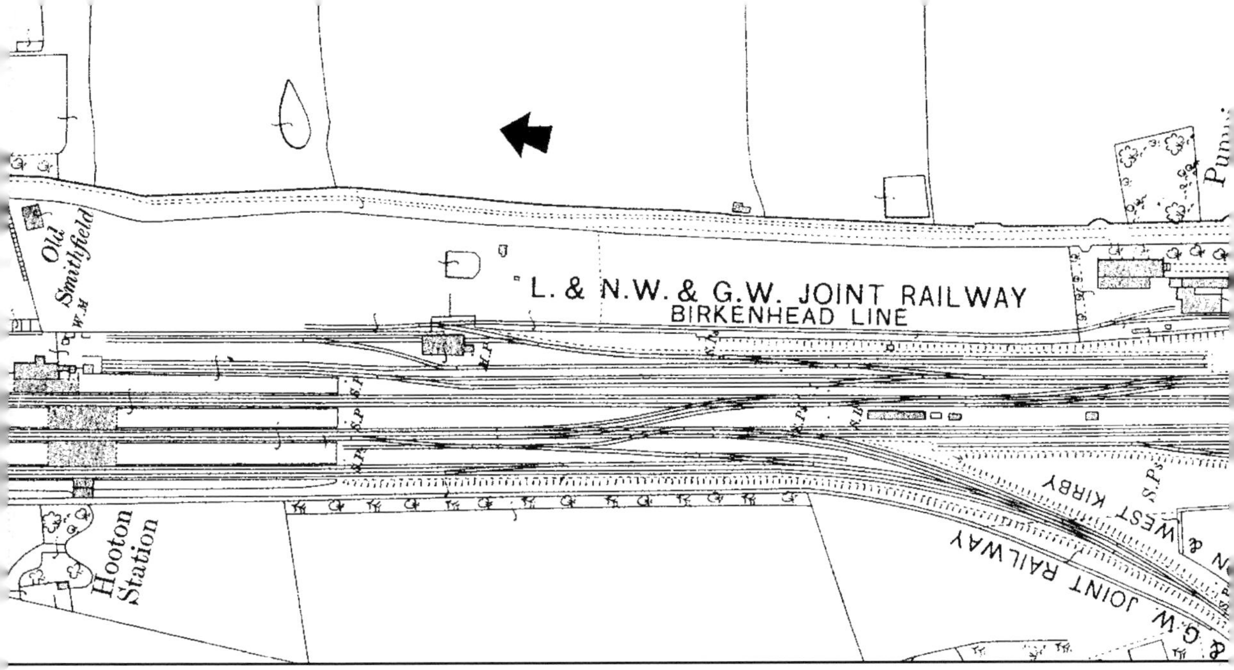

30. A Webb 3-cylinder compound 2-4-0 runs in with a local train from Chester, bound for Birkenhead. The north end of the engine shed is on the left. Part of it may have been used for goods from an early date. Included is South Junction box, which had 128 levers, these being reduced to 80 in 1973. (R.S.Carpenter coll.)

31. The two platforms on the left were used by West Kirby trains and, on the right, a train stands at the bay platform for Helsby trains. The white jib of the 2½ ton capacity crane is visible. This is the view from the box, which became plain Hooton on 9th December 1973, when North Box closed. That had 90 levers and is on the left page of the map. (Lens of Sutton coll.)

32. Running through on the passenger line in about 1930 is LMS "Crab" 2-6-0 no. 13233. The wagons on the right carry their owners names, a practice which was discontinued with the advent of World War II. (Lens of Sutton coll.)

33. Two 2-6-4Ts face Birkenhead in about 1954, but no details survive. The distant one has steam in strange places. Goods traffic ceased here on 2nd March 1964. (Milepost 92½)

34. Arriving with the 5.10pm Stanlow to Birkenhead on 2nd June 1961 is 2-6-2T no. 84005. The gas lamps are Sugg's Rochester pattern, which were shadow free. Some of the nearby RAF airfields were acquired by Vauxhall Motors in 1962. Quadruple track reduction followed thus: Hooton North Junction to Rock Ferry - Down Fast abolished 21st July 1968; Up Fast downgraded to Up Goods 15th December 1968 and abolished 2nd December 1973. (H.C.Casserley)

35. No. 47123 was photographed on 22nd August 1984, after it had run round its train of tankers in transit from Ellesmere Port to Amlwch, in Anglesey. There is evidence of two buffer stops on the right and one on the left. The loop can be seen in the distance, but its buffers cannot. (D.H.Mitchell)

36. The headboard says all that is needed on 30th September 1985, by which time one short black canopy had replaced the extensive array from earlier days. The two through platforms were for seven cars and the bay took six. The EMU is described in caption 55. (Milepost 92½)

37. Cobbled paving was to be seen in the 1980s, along with modern lighting. The building continued to serve its intended function. The signal box was replaced by a Portakabin on 18th May 1985 and this received a new panel in 2008. (A.Dudman coll.)

38. It is 2nd May 1988 and the centenary celebrations of Lever Bros Port Sunlight Works were proceeding. Preserved EMU no. 29896 was working a Hooton to Port Sunlight shuttle service on that day. The DMU on the right was running between here and Chester. (T.Heavyside)

39. Seen on 25th October 1990, Hooton was the southern limit of Merseyrail electrification from 1985 until 1993. In this northward view, a class 508 electric unit from Liverpool has terminated at platform 2 on the left. A 30 year old class 108 set forms the half hourly connecting service from Chester to Ellesmere Port and Helsby at non-electrified platform 1. This line was the down fast following quadrupling, but by now had been lifted north of the station leaving a south facing bay. The station building is adjacent to the former up fast line. This also had been abolished beyond the station limits, leaving a run round siding only. (A.C.Hartless)

40. Pacer no. 142011 waits close to the buffers on 19th August 1992. The platform on the right was not then used by passenger trains. Work started on a new footbridge with lifts in June 2010. The main building housed the ticket office and a shop in 2012. (M.Turvey)

EASTHAM RAKE

41. Photographed on 23rd July 2001, the station had opened on 3rd April 1995. The up platform utilised the formation of the former fast lines and is to the right of the picture as no. 508127 arrives with the 15.04 Liverpool Central to Chester. The station is a good example of late twentieth century railway architecture with waiting shelters combining low maintenance with visual appeal, and gently angled footbridge slopes to assist access for wheelchairs. The traditional clocks are a notable feature, post-dating the digital displays of the 1980s. (A.C.Hartless)

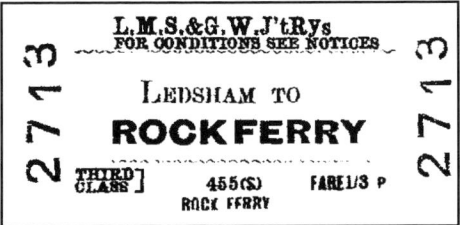

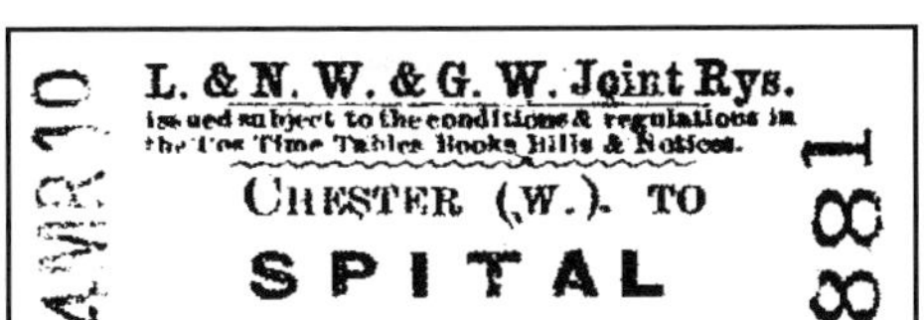

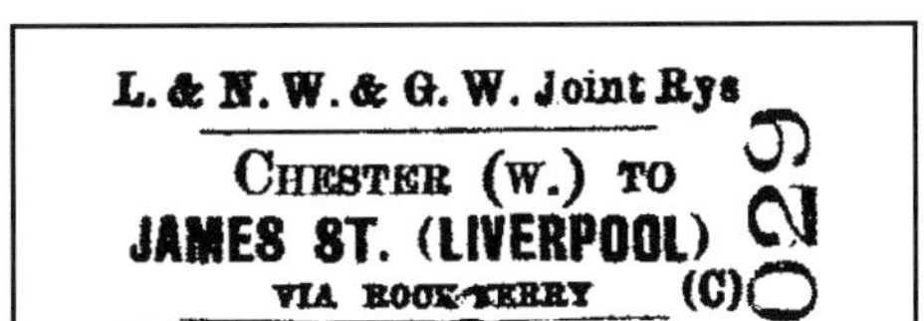

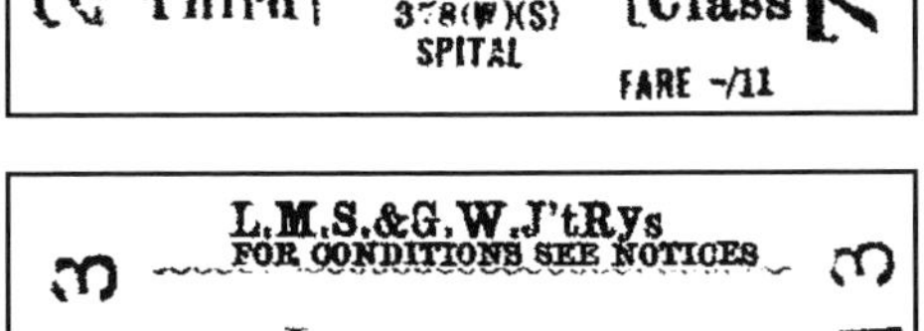

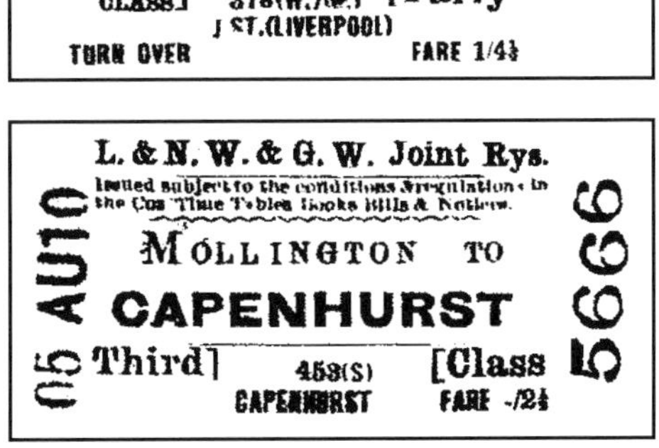

42. Shortly afterwards, no. 507007 is seen rearwards from the footbridge departing as the 15.20 Chester to Liverpool. The down side shelter appears to be identical to its opposite number. The formation of the former fast lines is discernible to the right of the running lines. (A.C.Hartless)

43. This is a roadside view of the station building on the same day. A plaque affixed records the official opening of the station on 7th June 1995. 'Rake' is a north country alternative to 'road'; Eastham itself is about a mile to the east. The area in between was open country when the railway was built, but has been subsequently filled by low density housing. (A.C.Hartless)

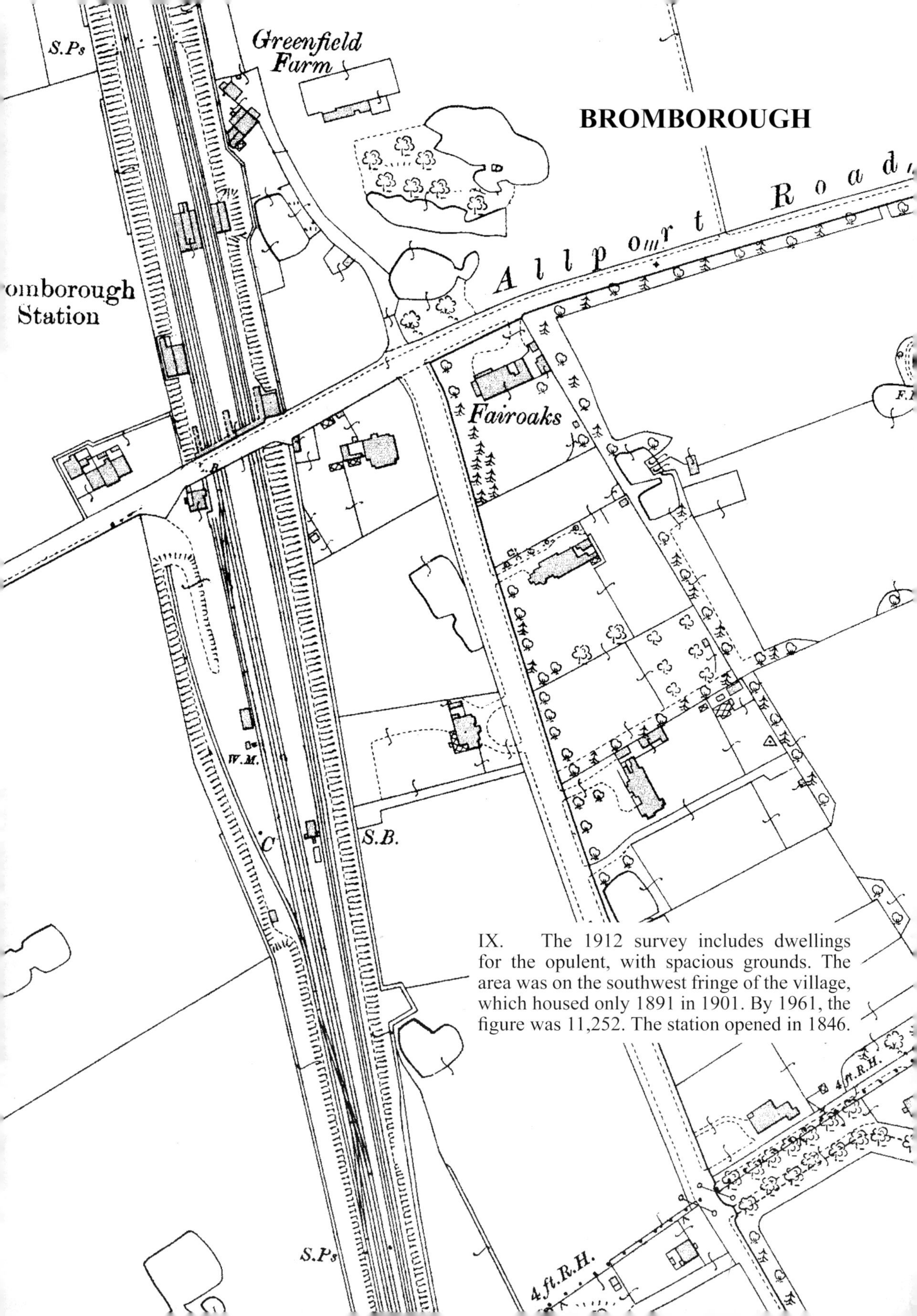

IX. The 1912 survey includes dwellings for the opulent, with spacious grounds. The area was on the southwest fringe of the village, which housed only 1891 in 1901. By 1961, the figure was 11,252. The station opened in 1846.

44. The original lines are on the left of this northward view from about 1910. The island platform and its central building would still be fairly new. (Stations UK)

45. The access to the goods yard is in the foreground as 2-6-4T no. 42570 runs towards Chester on 18th August 1958. The photographer is on the dock and behind him is a 4-ton crane in the yard, which closed on 30th October 1965. (R.S.Carpenter coll.)

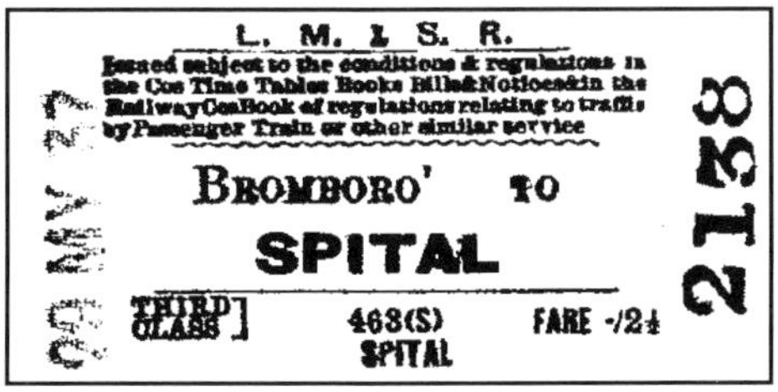

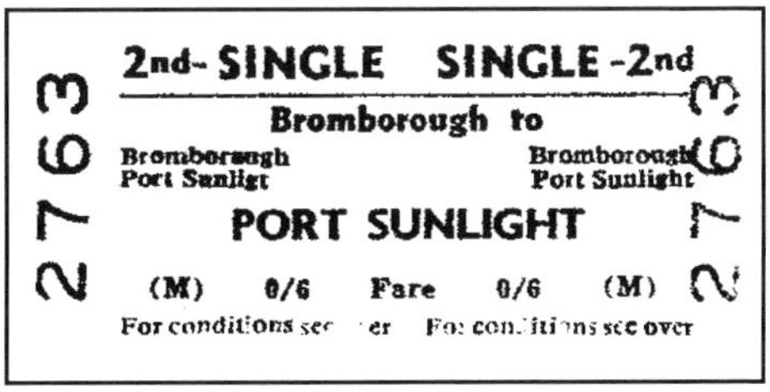

46. Proceeding towards Birkenhead on 2nd June 1961 is 2-6-4T no. 42569 with the 6.35pm from Chester. The entrance building is on the skyline on the right. (R.M.Casserley)

47. The entrance is top right in this 1967 picture, which includes 2-6-4T no. 42587 accelerating fiercely. The gradient post indicates that it is level to Hooton. (Stations UK)

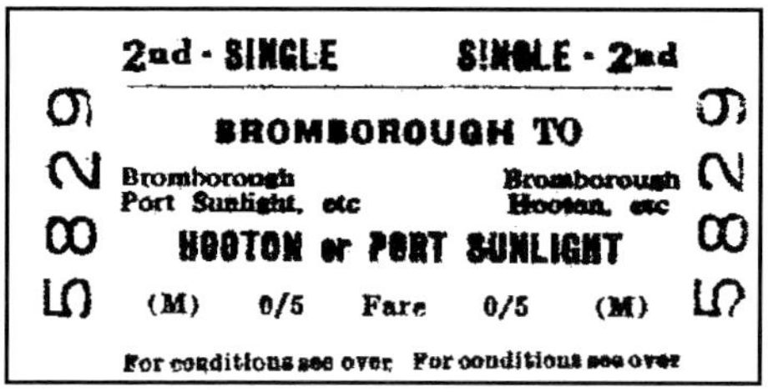

5829 2nd - SINGLE SINGLE - 2nd 5829
BROMBOROUGH TO
Bromborough Port Sunlight, etc / Bromborough Hooton, etc
HOOTON or PORT SUNLIGHT
(M) 0/5 Fare 0/5 (M)
For conditions see over For conditions see over

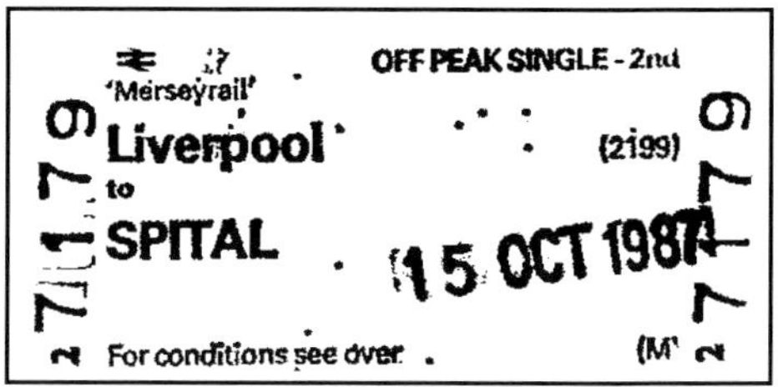

'Merseyrail' OFF PEAK SINGLE - 2nd
Liverpool (2199)
to
SPITAL 15 OCT 1987
For conditions see over (M)

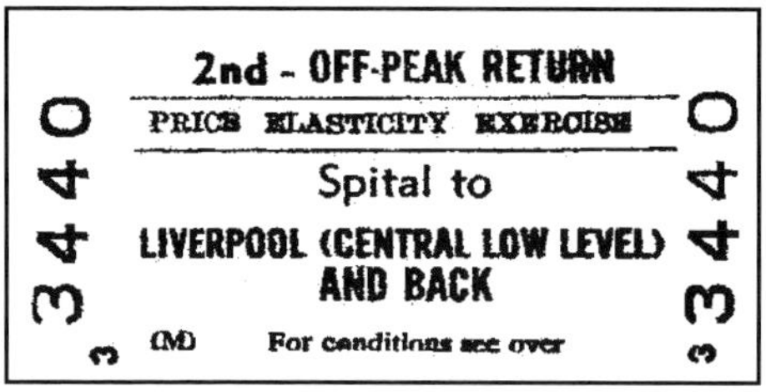

3440 2nd - OFF-PEAK RETURN 3440
PRICE ELASTICITY EXERCISE
Spital to
LIVERPOOL (CENTRAL LOW LEVEL)
AND BACK
(M) For conditions see over

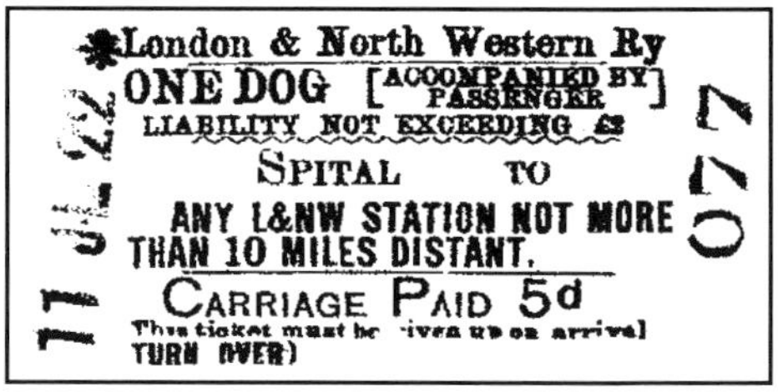

London & North Western Ry
ONE DOG [ACCOMPANIED BY PASSENGER]
LIABILITY NOT EXCEEDING £5
SPITAL TO
ANY L&NW STATION NOT MORE THAN 10 MILES DISTANT.
CARRIAGE PAID 5d
This ticket must be given up on arrival
TURN OVER) 077

48. The Wirral Railway Circle hired a train to tour the Wirral lines on 1st April 1978 and no. 25201 is passing through with it. Semaphore signals are still to be seen, as the 36-lever signal box did not close until 18th May 1985. (T.Heavyside)

49. This northward view is from the down side as no. 508126 arrives on 25th October 1990, with an early afternoon Liverpool Central to Hooton service. The more distant of the two bridges in the background is at Bromborough Rake. (A.C.Hartless)

50. The station entrance in Allport Road has a restrained mock Tudor character. It remains in use, despite another station opening nearby in 1985. (A.C.Hartless)

BROMBOROUGH RAKE

51. A class 508 EMU runs in on 25th October 1990 with an early afternoon Hooton to Liverpool Central service. The station opened on 30th September 1985, the same day that electric services were extended from Rock Ferry to Hooton. The down side shelter is commodious, but totally lacking in style, whilst the up side shelter is merely small and totally lacking in style. Close inspection of the left hand side of the bridge reveals the original arch that spanned the fast lines. (A.C.Hartless)

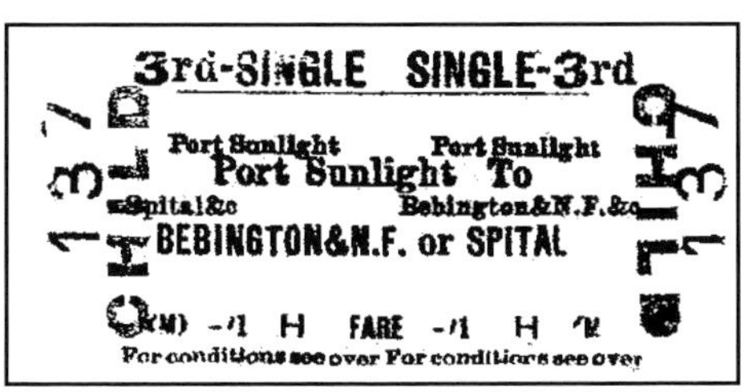

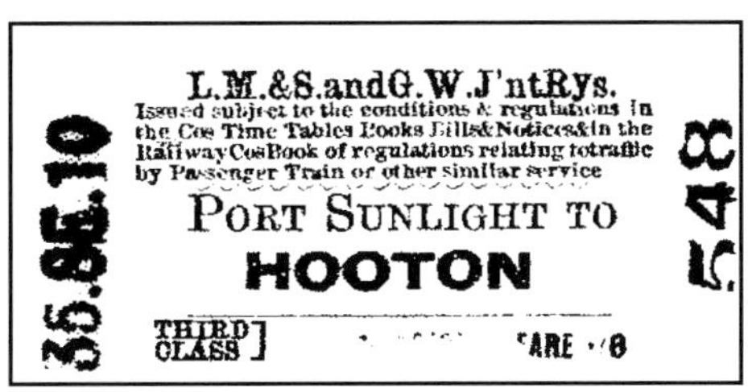

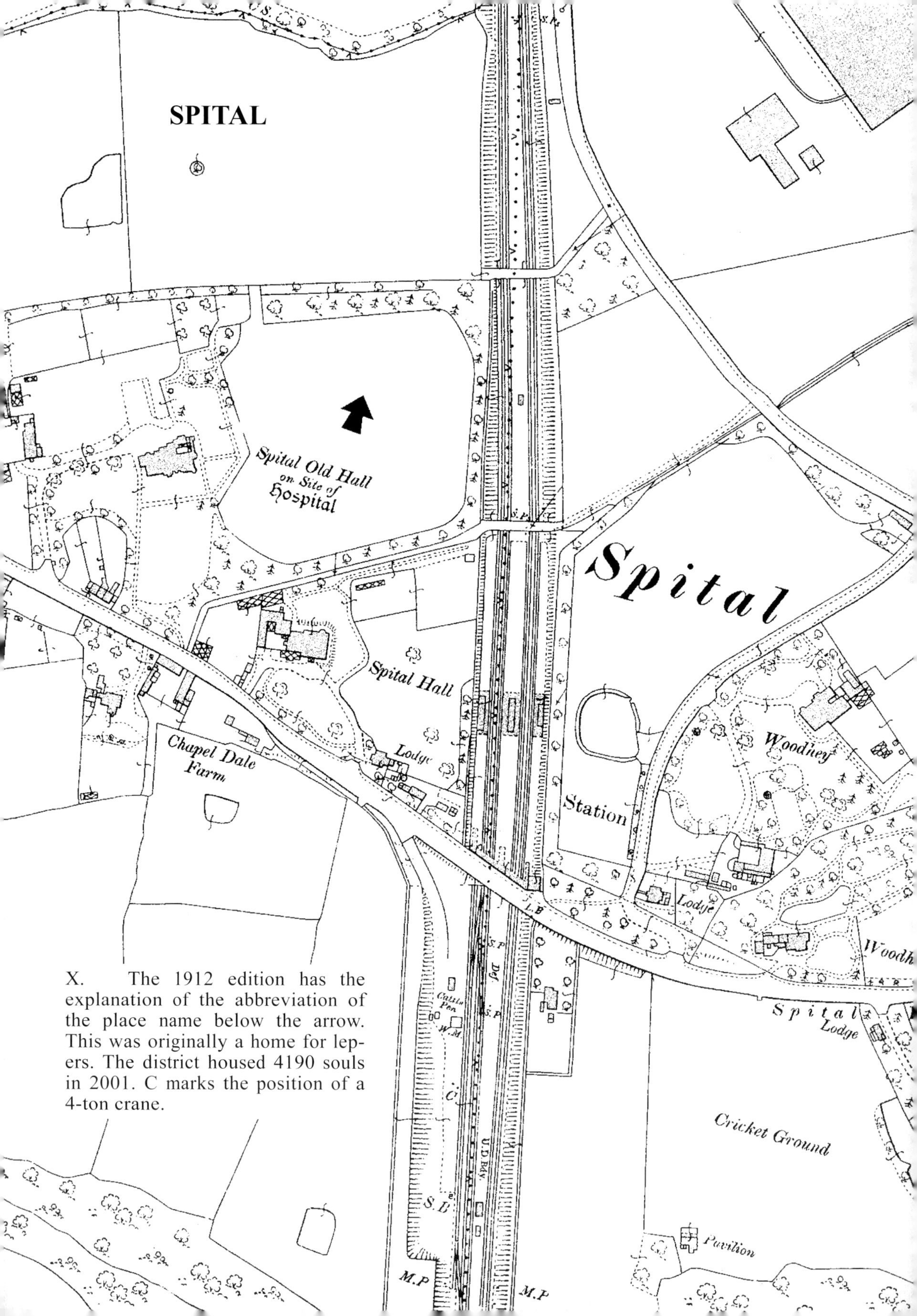

X. The 1912 edition has the explanation of the abbreviation of the place name below the arrow. This was originally a home for lepers. The district housed 4190 souls in 2001. C marks the position of a 4-ton crane.

52. The 10.5am Birkenhead Woodside to Llandudno is seen behind 2-6-4T no. 40209, sometime in 1958. The grounds of Spital Hall are on the left. The station had opened in June 1846. (R.S.Carpenter coll.)

53. Poor light prevailed when this 1960 panorama was recorded. The goods yard was beyond the bridge and was in use until 3rd August 1964. Goods traffic began here in October 1927. (Stations UK)

54. No. 508113 formed the 13.10 Hooton to Liverpool on 30th October 1985 and passes a colour light signal. The nearby 36-lever signal box had closed on 25th June 1972. (T.Heavyside)

55. The other direction was photographed on 30th April 1988 as the National Railway Museum's EMU passes, during the Port Sunlight Centenary weekend. Top quality track was now in place. The rear car is no. 28361. Both were disposed of by the NRM in October 2011 and a sad story followed, see www.class502.org.uk. (T.Heavyside)

PORT SUNLIGHT

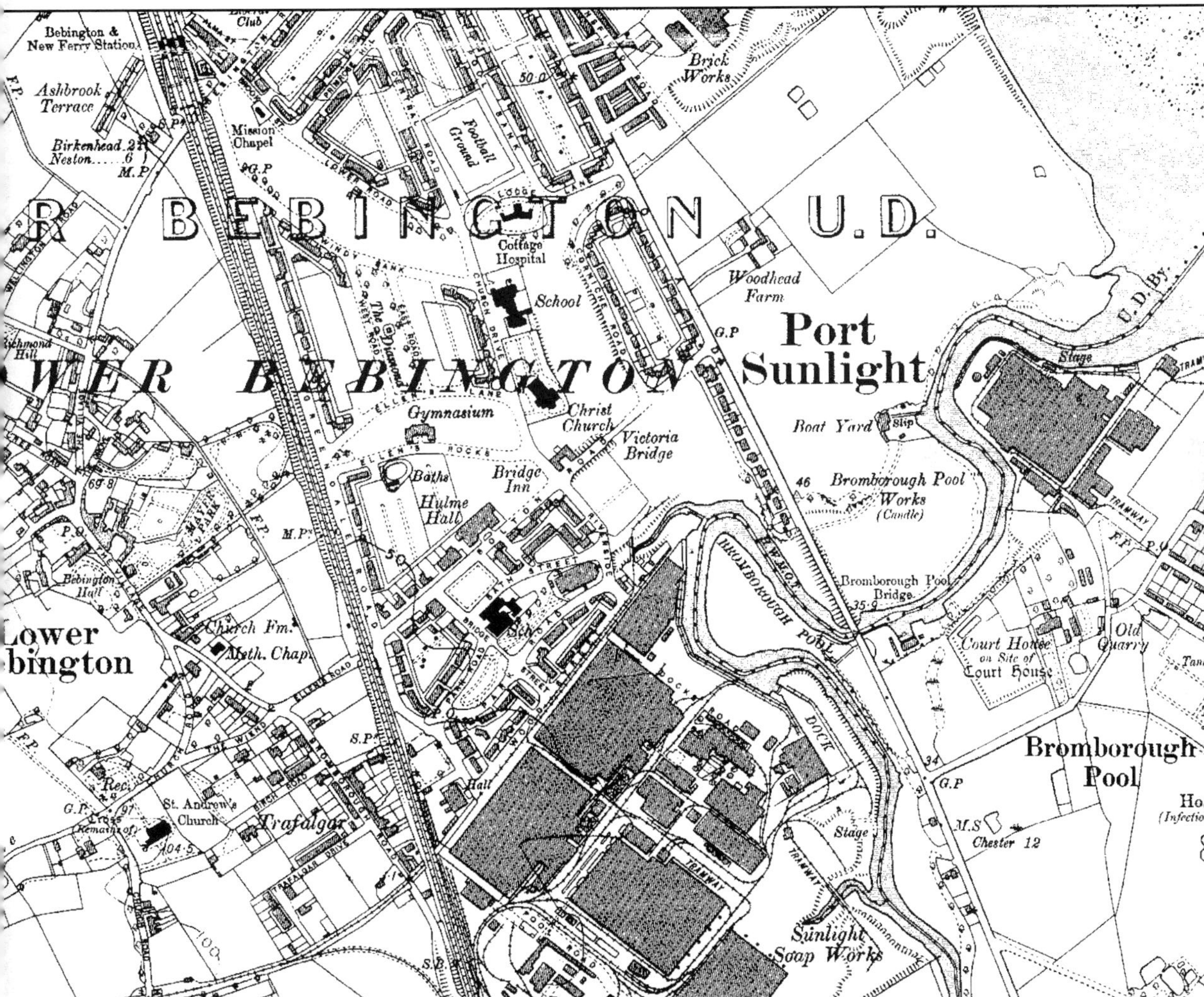

XI. The 1913 map at 6ins to 1 mile does not include the station, as it did not open until 4th May 1914. It was for the use of factory workers only until 9th May 1927 and was situated to the right of the word **Trafalgar**. Lever Bros. Ltd., soap factory is shaded. The line lower left ran to a quarry. The next station north is at the top of the map. The company had a fleet of Barclay 0-6-0Ts, with brake vans endorsed LBL. The factory was started in 1888 and its first locomotive arrived in 1891. The estate later accommodated other businesses.

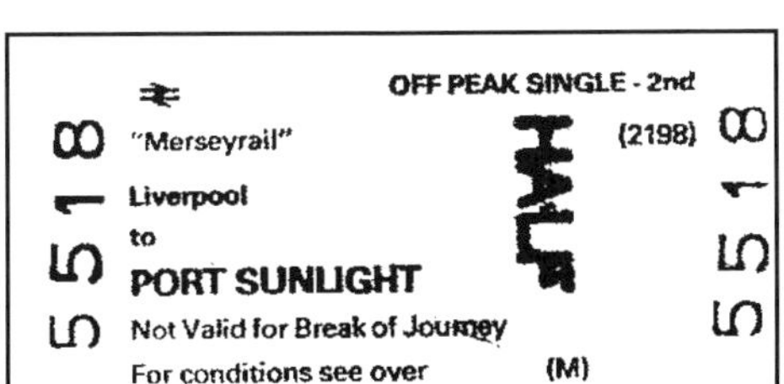

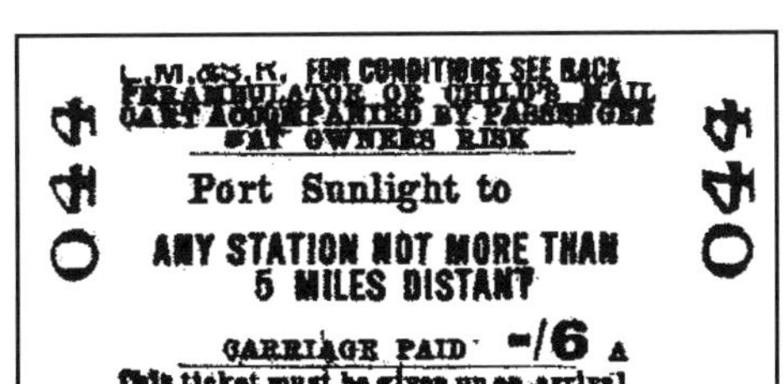

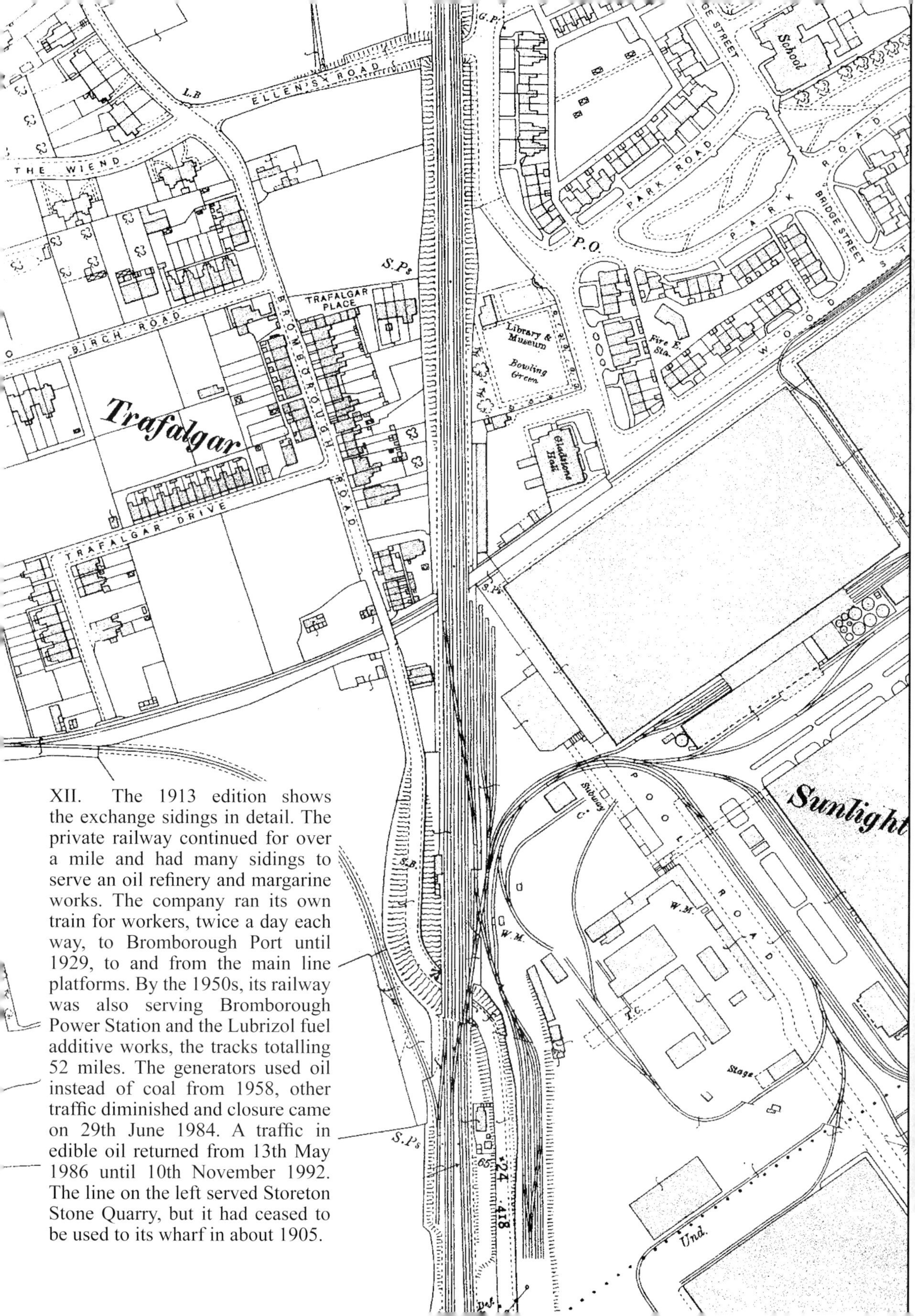

XII. The 1913 edition shows the exchange sidings in detail. The private railway continued for over a mile and had many sidings to serve an oil refinery and margarine works. The company ran its own train for workers, twice a day each way, to Bromborough Port until 1929, to and from the main line platforms. By the 1950s, its railway was also serving Bromborough Power Station and the Lubrizol fuel additive works, the tracks totalling 52 miles. The generators used oil instead of coal from 1958, other traffic diminished and closure came on 29th June 1984. A traffic in edible oil returned from 13th May 1986 until 10th November 1992. The line on the left served Storeton Stone Quarry, but it had ceased to be used to its wharf in about 1905.

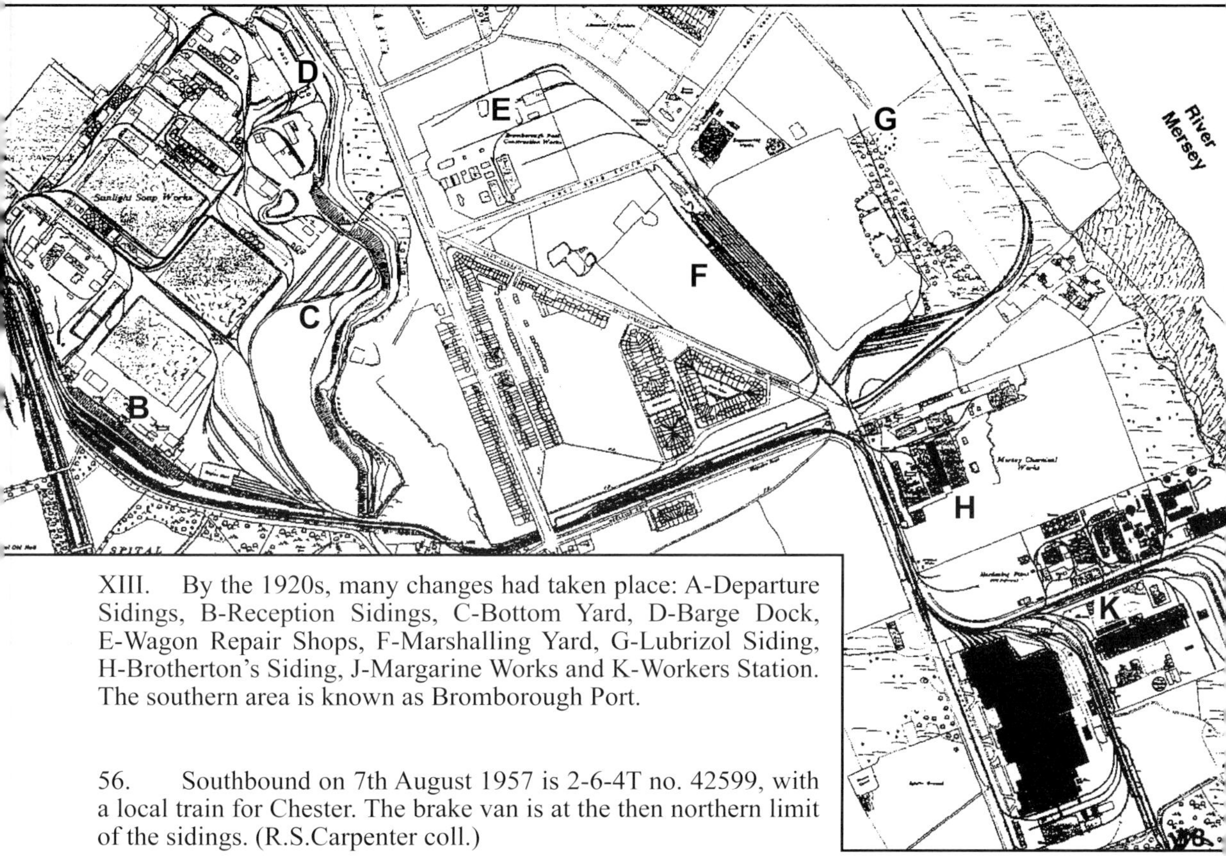

XIII. By the 1920s, many changes had taken place: A-Departure Sidings, B-Reception Sidings, C-Bottom Yard, D-Barge Dock, E-Wagon Repair Shops, F-Marshalling Yard, G-Lubrizol Siding, H-Brotherton's Siding, J-Margarine Works and K-Workers Station. The southern area is known as Bromborough Port.

56. Southbound on 7th August 1957 is 2-6-4T no. 42599, with a local train for Chester. The brake van is at the then northern limit of the sidings. (R.S.Carpenter coll.)

57. Seen in the 1960s, the platforms were notable for taking 14 coaches each, but the lack of an island platform presented operational difficulties. A subway was provided for passengers in 1920. (Stations UK)

58. The 11.25 Chester to Rock Ferry is pictured on 22nd August 1974, along with the 50-lever LNWR signal box, which was in use until 2nd November 1986. It was initially known as Lever Bros Sidings box. The wooden platforms were replaced in 1969, but they now take only six coaches. (T.Heavyside)

59. The Port Sunlight centenary event involved many attractions over its three days. Normally running on the Severn Valley Railway, 2-6-2T no. 4566 was photographed on 30th April 1988. (T.Heavyside)

60. Recorded on 2nd May 1988 was 0-6-0T no. 7298 from the Llangollen Railway, running on the other end of the same train on the private railway. This once conveyed caustic soda and palm oil from coconut kernels in quantity. (T. Heavyside)

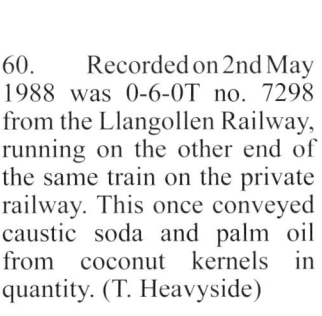

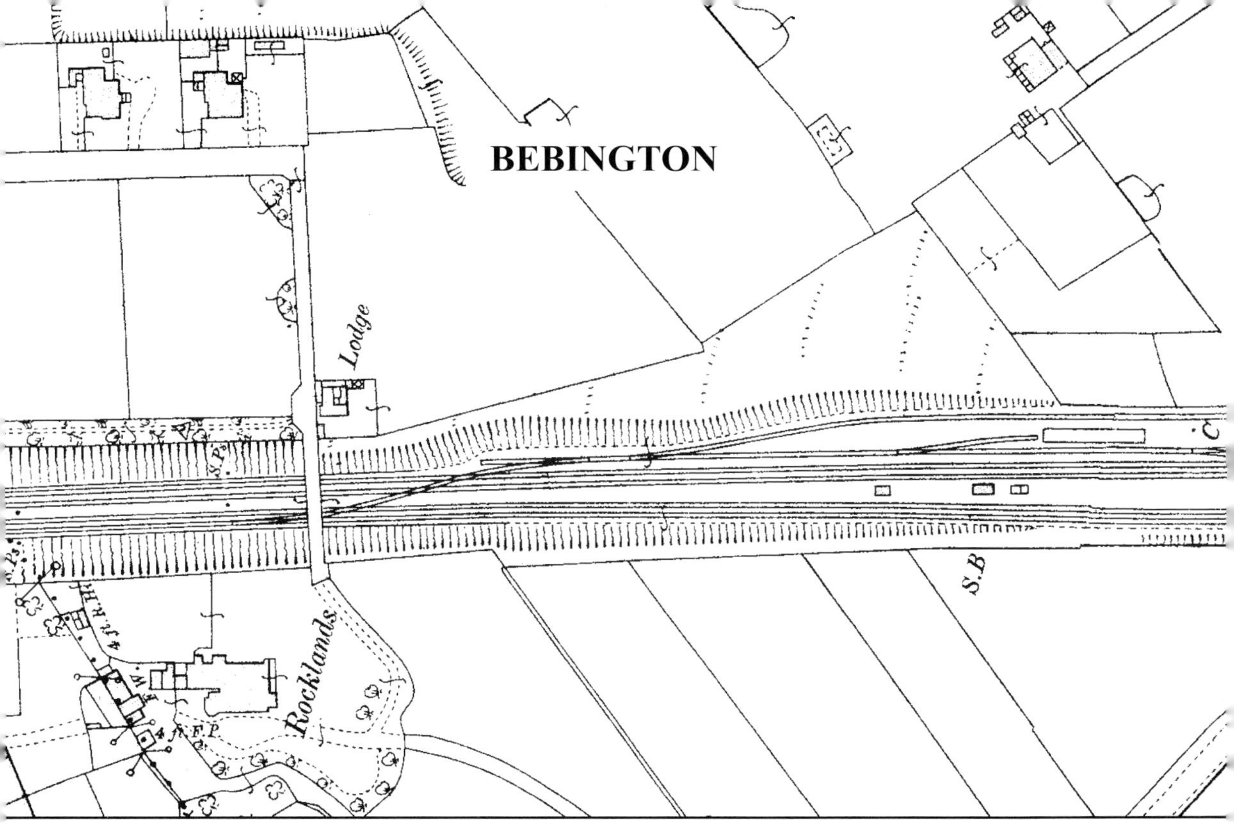

XIV. The 1913 edition includes the suffix, which was added on 1st May 1895 and was used until 6th May 1974. The small goods yard is shown to have a crane; it was rated at 10 tons. Freight ceased on 30th October 1965.

61. This northward panorama is from about 1930 and includes access to the subway, the roof of which is in the foreground. In the distance is the signal box, which had 36 levers and functioned until 18th September 1974, when quadruple track came to an end here. (Stations UK)

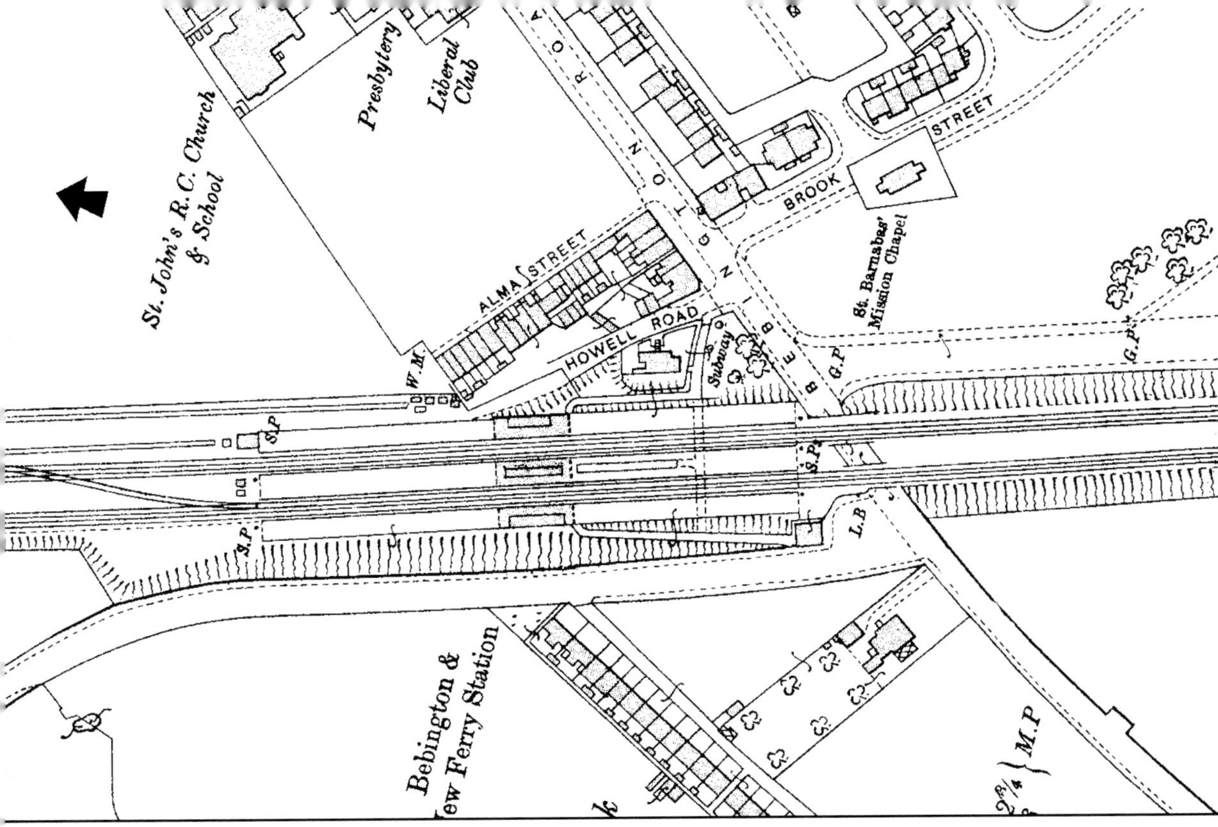

62. The western pair of tracks were retained and are seen as no. 508113 leads a six-coach train on the 13.56 Liverpool Central to Hooton on 5th April 1986. The down side building has been demolished except for the rear wall, and a draughty looking shelter put in its place. The up side has been left devoid of structures. The graceful arch in the background is an accommodation bridge, which spanned all four tracks. (A.C.Hartless)

ROCK FERRY

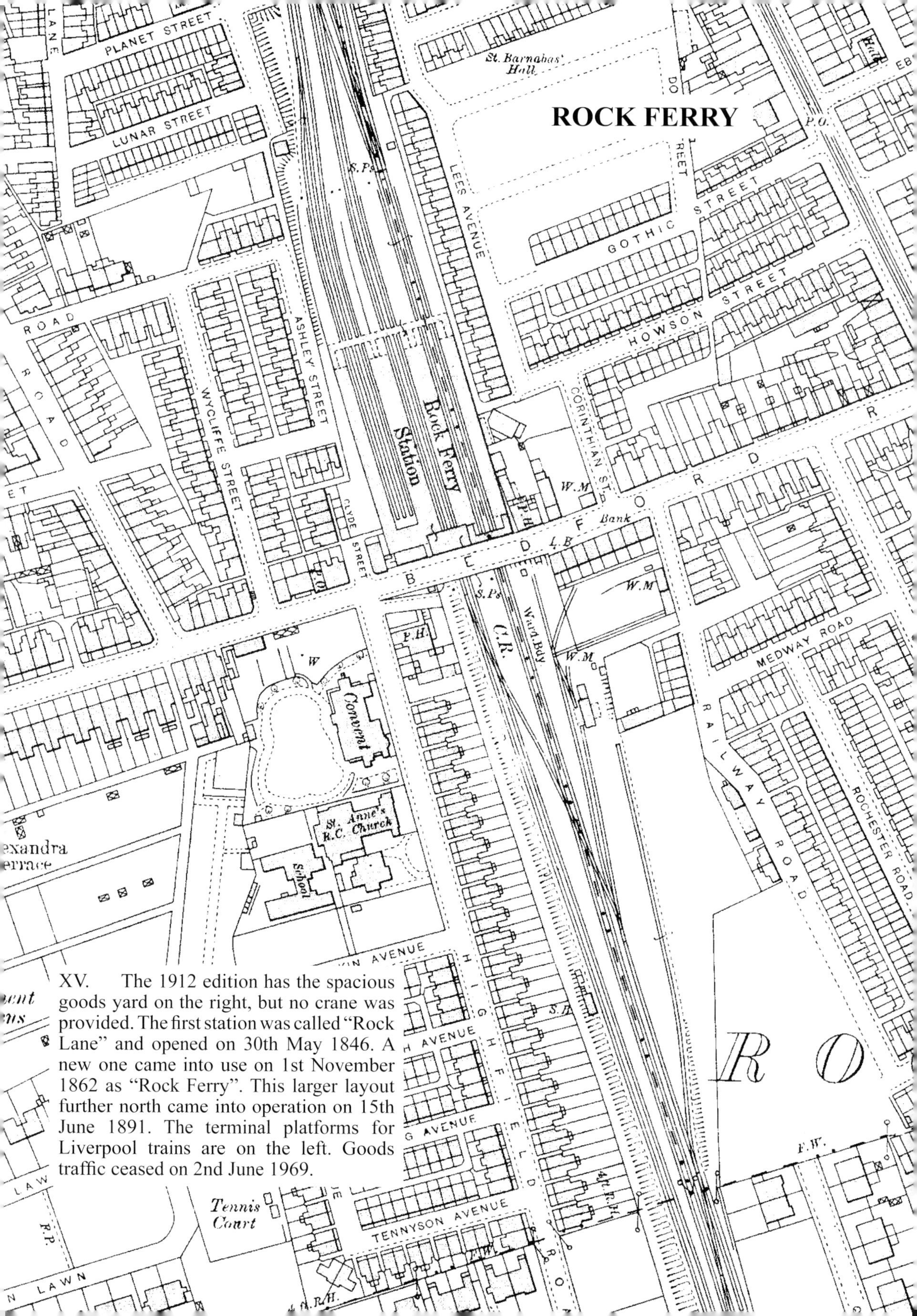

XV. The 1912 edition has the spacious goods yard on the right, but no crane was provided. The first station was called "Rock Lane" and opened on 30th May 1846. A new one came into use on 1st November 1862 as "Rock Ferry". This larger layout further north came into operation on 15th June 1891. The terminal platforms for Liverpool trains are on the left. Goods traffic ceased on 2nd June 1969.

63. A Mersey Railway train runs into platform 5 to terminate its service from Liverpool, sometime before the electrification of 1903. The massive pipe on the 4-4-2T was to permit condensing of exhaust steam in the water tank, during passage through the tunnels. (A.M.Davies coll.)

64. Here is an example of the replacement electric stock at the same platform. The centre road was for engine release and one crossover had been retained after electrification for no known reason. (Lens of Sutton coll.)

65. The 5.45pm Birkenhead Woodside to Helsby is on the slow line on 2nd June 1961, hauled by 2-6-4T no. 42212. A fast train passes through platform 2 in the other direction. (H.C.Casserley)

66. Seen on the same day is the footbridge shown on the map. The lifts were a later addition. The span over the terminal lines and platforms is on the right. Platforms 1 and 2 were abolished on 15th December 1968 and the others were renumbered. (R.M.Casserley)

XVI. This extract continues north from the previous one and has the signal box at the bottom. It is clear at the top that there are six tracks. The four on the right go to the Woodside terminus, while the other two curve towards Green Lane.

67. The 10.50 to Liverpool was recorded on 1st April 1978, with the Chester lines on the left. This was a busy interchange station between diesel and electric services for many years. (T.Heavyside)

68. No. M28392M is waiting to return to Liverpool from platform 3 on 14th August 1983. The signal box replaced the one seen earlier on 12th May 1957. It had a 60-lever frame, which was superseded by a panel and a 10-lever frame on 19th May 1985. It closed completely on 18th September 1994. (T.Heavyside)

69. The approach to the platform is seen minutes earlier. This illustration reveals that there were then no tracks north of platforms 1 and 2. They had been effectively bay platforms since 1968 and remained so until electrification to Hooton in 1985. A footpath on the trackbed linked platforms 1 to 3 in that period; handrails still appear in picture 71. (T.Heavyside)

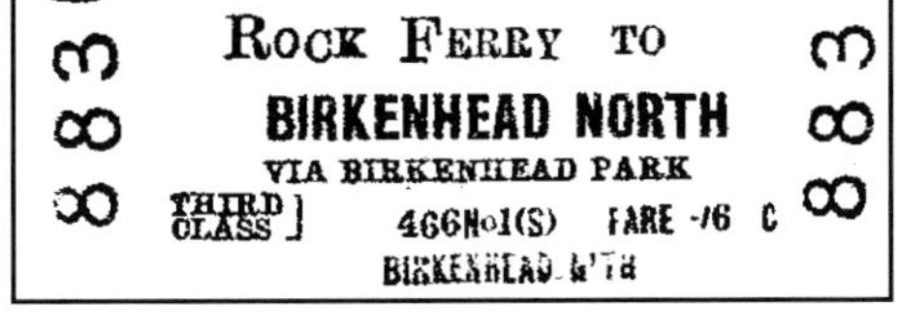

70. The preserved EMU seen in picture 55 was in action again on 6th April 1986 in connection with Birkenhead North Depot Open Day. A scheduled train for the Liverpool Loop is at platform 4. Note that the release road had gone, long obsolete. (T.Heavyside)

71. The 10-lever frame mentioned earlier was for the goods line on which no. 33051 is about to run on 18th January 1986. It would take the special train along the Mersey Docks & Harbour Company's lines, which linked with the electrified tracks at Bidston East Junction. Hertfordshire Railtours named the train "Wirral Withershins" and it ran from and to London Victoria, with no. 33062 on the other end. (Milepost 92½)

GREEN LANE

72. Tranmere station, open from 30th May 1846, was renamed Lime Kiln Lane in 1853 and closed in October 1857. A little further north, Green Lane was opened by the Mersey Railway on 1st February 1886. It was at a low level, being on the approach to the Mersey Tunnel. The nameboard carried "For Lairdside" in 2002. South of the station is Green Lane Tunnel (59yds) and north of it is Hinderton Field Tunnel (497yds). (A.M.Davies coll.)

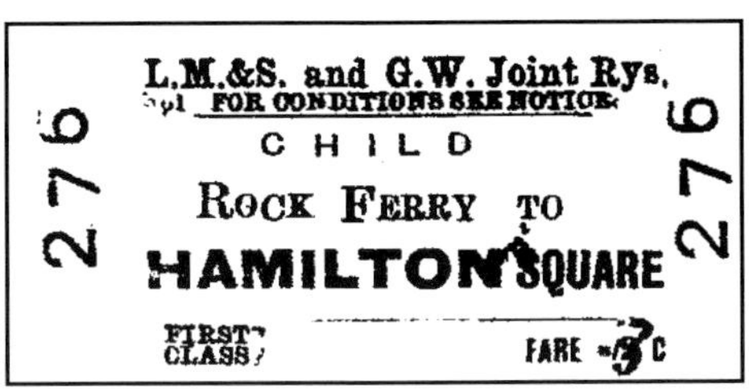

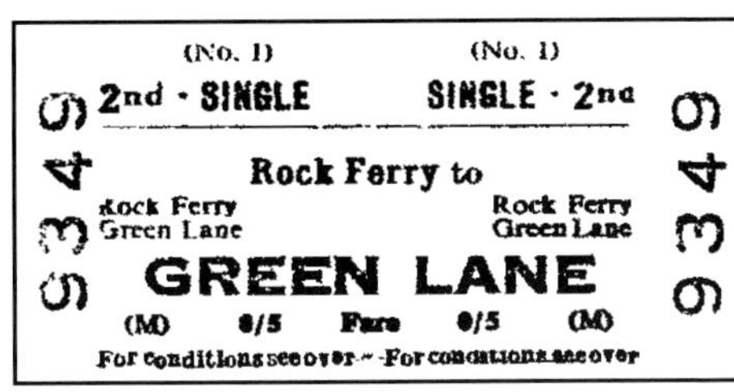

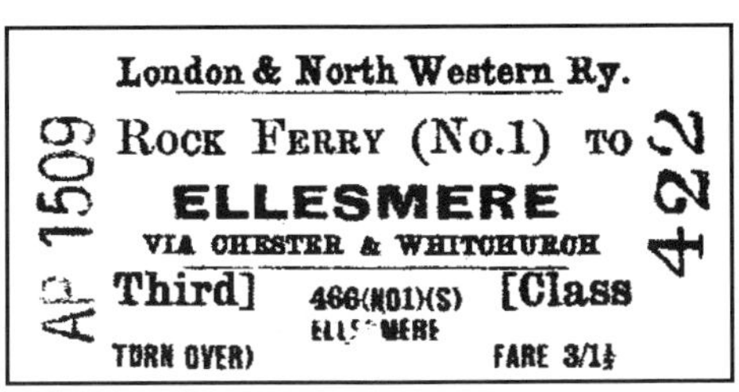

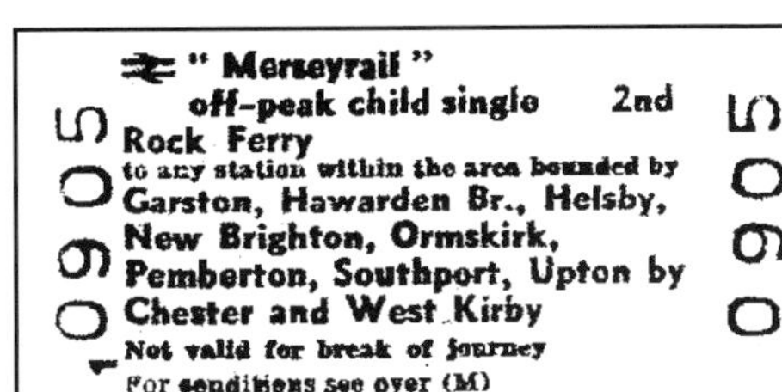

SOUTH OF BIRKENHEAD

XVII. Green Lane and its station are near the bottom of this 1913 map at 5ins to 1 mile. The main line continues north and divides near Town Station. It then goes under much of Chester Street to reach the terminus at Woodside. Above the words MERSEY RAILWAY is the joint engine shed and above that is Central Station. The line north of that is under Haymarket and Hamilton Street, at the top of which is Hamilton Square Station. The platforms here are very deep, being close to the start of the Mersey Tunnel. South of Woodside (right) is Monk's Ferry (Coal Stage). This had been the passenger terminus before Woodside opened in 1878 and half the length of the branch can be seen to be in tunnel.

Engine Shed

73. The GWR had a three-road shed here until 1878, when the joint shed was created, each half having eight roads. On the left is part of the ex-LNWR side, with its choice of ventilators, and is seen on 20th June 1948. Most of the roof was of the north light type, preferred by the GWR. (B.W.L.Brooksbank)

Extract from Bradshaw's Guide for 1866.
(Reprinted by Middleton Press 2011)

BIRKENHEAD,

A telegraph station.

HOTELS.—The Woodside, Adelphi, and Castle.

This place contains a population of 51,649, chiefly engaged in shipbuilding; large docks of 150 acres, made by Rendel, and opened in August, 1847; 4 chapels, court house, St. Aidan's college, founded in 1849; gas and water works, Abattoir pier Market place, 430 feet long; St. Mary's church which overlooks the river was part of a restored abbey, ruins of a priory founded in 1150 by Hamon de Massey, 2 churches, fine park and great square. In the vicinity are Seacombe, Egremont, Leasowe Castle, and New Brighton, with the Blackrock Lighthouse and Bidstone Light.

74. A close up on 20th April 1954 includes 0-4-2T no. 1457 centre stage. The shed was coded by BR as 6C, but it became 8H in September 1963. The main use of the pits was for the reception of ash, raked out of the ashpans of the locomotives. (H.C.Casserley)

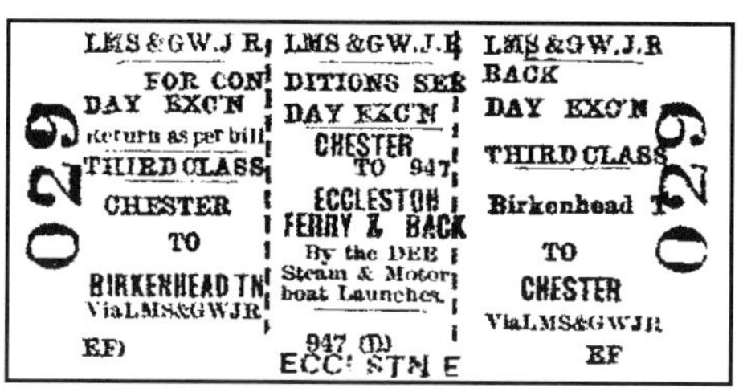

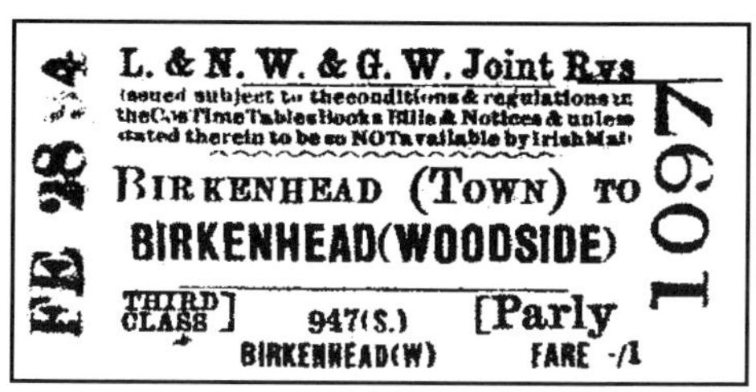

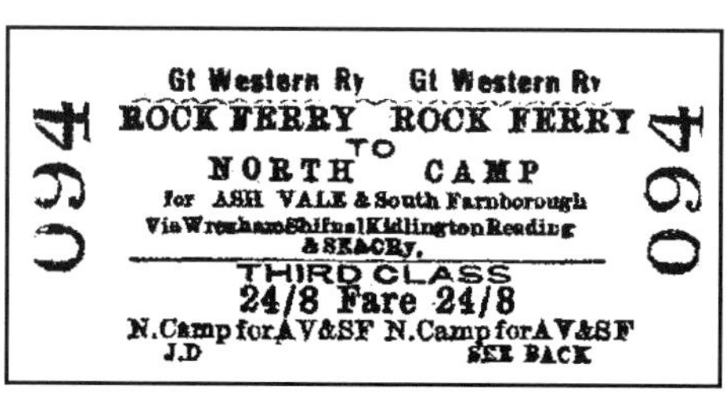

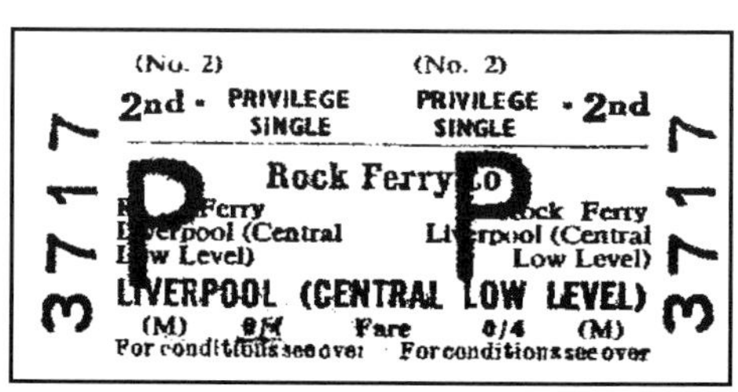

75. Each company had its own turntable (see map), but eventually a single one was provided at the south end of the site. No. 6863 *Dolhywel Grange* was recorded on it in June 1959. (D.K.Jones coll.)

76. Resting on 18th February 1966 are nos 48613, 90351 and 92048. The boundary wall between the two halves of the shed was still evident. The GWR had 43 locomotives allocated here in 1947. The total in 1950 was 93 and by 1959 it was down to 56. (T.Heavyside)

77. Out of steam on the same day were nos 92157 and 90351. Looking in the other direction we glimpse part of the coaling plant. Diesel shunters had been introduced as early as December 1955. (T.Heavyside)

78. It is 28th June 1966 and we can marvel at the coaling plant, completed in 1955. Entire wagons loaded with ten tons of coal were lifted up and tipped in. Nos 92160, 92089 and 48676 were in attendance. The shed closed operationally in November 1967. (T.Heavyside)

79. The buildings continued to be used for storage and are seen on 16th July 1985. Part of the ex-LNWR shed is on the left; it had been reroofed in 1938, having previously had the north-light system. The carriage shed is shown on the map, east of the engine shed. The curved sidings were for coach berthing. (T.Heavyside)

BIRKENHEAD TOWN

80. The station was in use from 1st January 1889 until 7th May 1945 and this northward view of it is from the 1930s. The original Grange Road terminus of the Birkenhead & Chester Railway had been behind the building on the left from 1840 to 1844. The line to Monk's Ferry branches right in front of the signal box and passes through the arch on the right and along under Ivy Street. The box closed on 8th August 1948. (Stations UK)

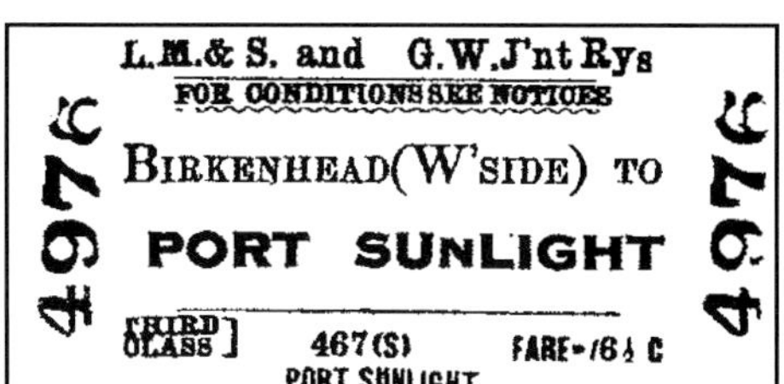

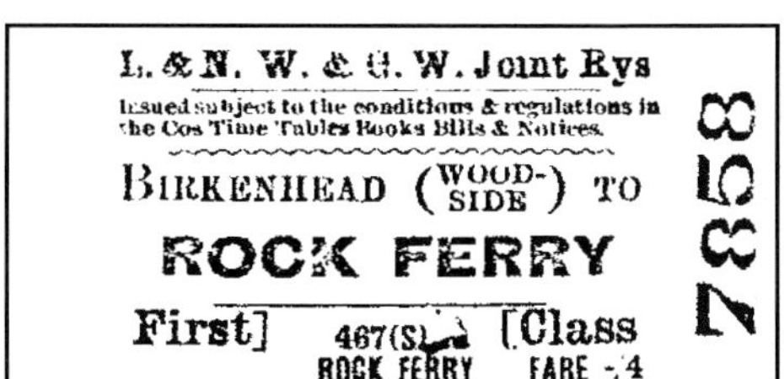

MONK'S FERRY

81. The waterfront terminus was used by passengers from 23rd October 1844 until 31st March 1878, when Woodside opened. However, the location continued to be used for coal, mainly for local ships, until 1967. This view from 1954 features the historic structure, which was soon to be demolished. (J.A.Peden)

XVIII. A 1910 diagram has the remains of the passenger station west of Church Street, its location being north of Ivy Street on the previous map. The ferry pier is on the right and the tunnel carrying the line to Laird's Shipyard runs under the street to it.

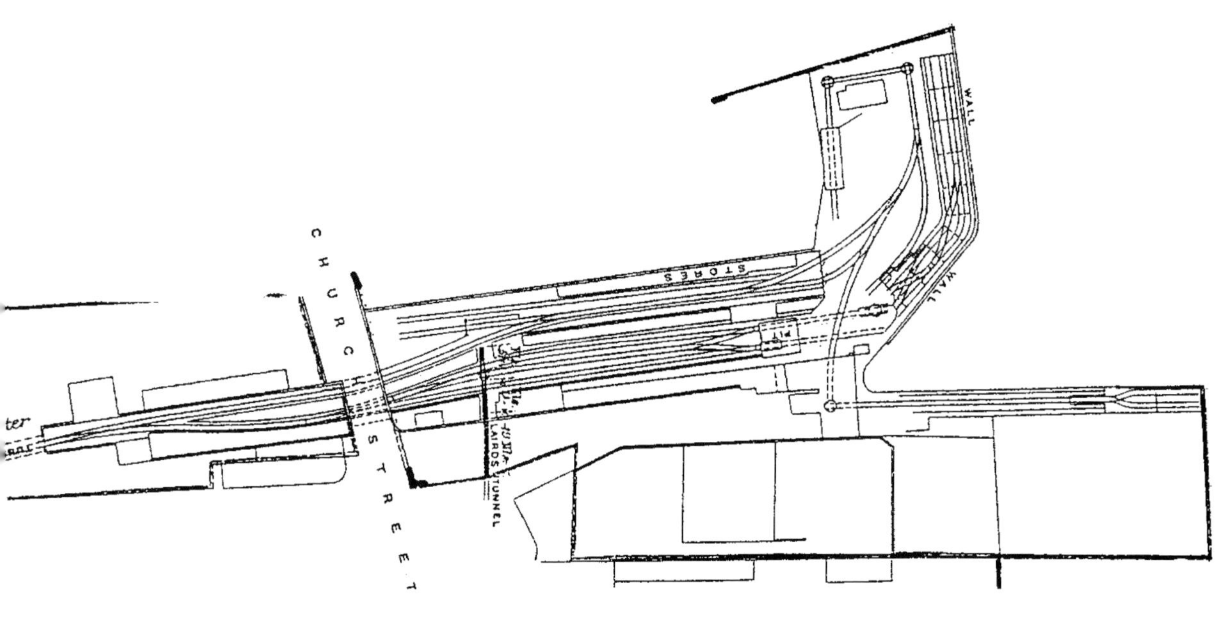

BIRKENHEAD CENTRAL

82. We return to the through lines and are north of the gasworks, with the Mersey Railway offering trains every few minutes to Liverpool and Rock Ferry in about 1924. This was the head office of the MR. (Stations UK)

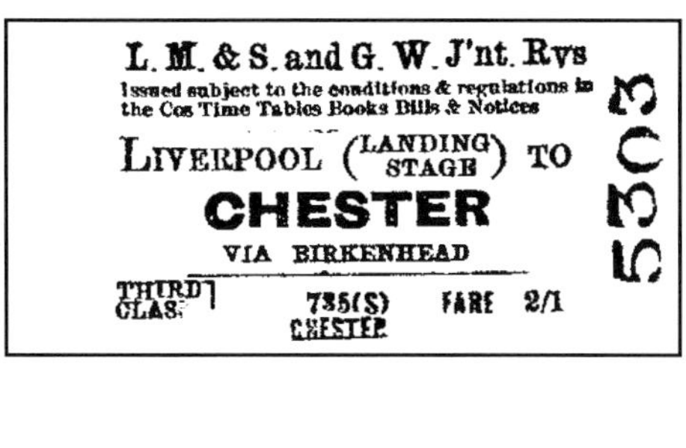

L. M. & S. and G. W. J'nt. Rys
Issued subject to the conditions & regulations in the Cos Time Tables Books Bills & Notices
LIVERPOOL (LANDING STAGE) TO
CHESTER
VIA BIRKENHEAD
THIRD CLASS 735(S) FARE 2/1
CHESTER
5303

L. & N. W. & G. W. Joint Rys.
LIVERPOOL (LANDING STAGE) TO
BEBINGTON
VIA BIRKENHEAD
Third] 735(S) [Class
BEBINGTON
TURN OVER) FARE -.4
4148

83. The north elevation was recorded at about the same time, along with regimented chimney pots. The Wirral Transport Museum once again operates trams through the streets of Birkenhead, between Egerton Wharf and Woodside Ferry. (Stations UK)

84. The carriage shed is seen from the up platform in about 1930. Birkenhead Corporation operated electric trams from 4th February 1901 until 17th July 1937, predating electric trains here by two years. (Stations UK)

85. A northward panorama includes a gas holder for location purposes and a large water tank for a link with the past steam age. It is apparent that the staff have their own footbridge. The shed with the curved roof had three tracks in it earlier, as did the one on the extreme right. The view is from 21st May 1961. (B.W.L.Brooksbank)

86. It is 14th August 1983 and a train has just emerged into daylight after a dull trip to Liverpool and back. It has passed through Haymarket Tunnel, which links with the Mersey Tunnel at Hamilton Square station. (T.Heavyside)

↓ 87. A closer look at the shed on the same day reveals the extent to which it was lengthened and the fact that the signs reveal overhead live rails within it. One exterior siding has since vanished. (T.Heavyside)

BIRKENHEAD WOODSIDE

89. GWR tank engines dominate this view from 19th April 1948. Rose Brae passes over the bridge, which adds to the gloom of the location, but it was demolished in 1961 and photographic opportunities were enhanced. (R.G.Nelson/T.Walsh coll.)

88. The ferry terminal is in the background in this view from about 1950. The side of the station is on the right, it containing the unintended main entrance in its wall. The plan had been to have it facing the waterfront and a splendid, elegant "Baronial Hall" was created to house the booking office windows, but it was only ever used for parcels. The tram terminus was built in the foreground and one now graces the scene again. (Stations UK)

90. The atmosphere created by this high vaulted roof and the echoes it generated were memorable and the music was often enhanced by passing ships with horns, hooters and whistles. Savour the scene in about 1960; it even includes a loading gauge. (Lens of Sutton coll.)

91. The other end of the fine structure can be enjoyed at about the same time. There were often six trains a day to Paddington, with Summer destinations including Llandudno, Brighton, Margate and Bournemouth. (Stations UK)

92. Church Street is over this bridge and a shipyard crane is on the left. In the gloom near it is a flat roofed BR signal box, which had 50 levers and was in use from 8th December 1955 until 5th November 1967, when the station closed completely. The box is behind the locomotive in the lower back cover picture. (Stations UK)

93. It is October 1965 and BR 4-6-0 no. 76020 waits to depart and it also waits for a good clean. Labour shortage and despondency caused many such problems in the sixties. Much stock was kept at Blackpool Street, where there was a signal box of that name. It had a 70-lever frame and lasted until 5th November 1967. (A.W.V.Mace/Milepost 92½)

94. The end is nigh and cameras abound on 4th March 1967, the last day of the Winter timetable and long distance running. On the left is no. 44730, a 4-6-0 working as station pilot, while behind the nameboard is 2-6-4T no. 42567 at the head of the 2.45pm to Paddington. It will take it only as far as Chester. (H.Ballantyne)

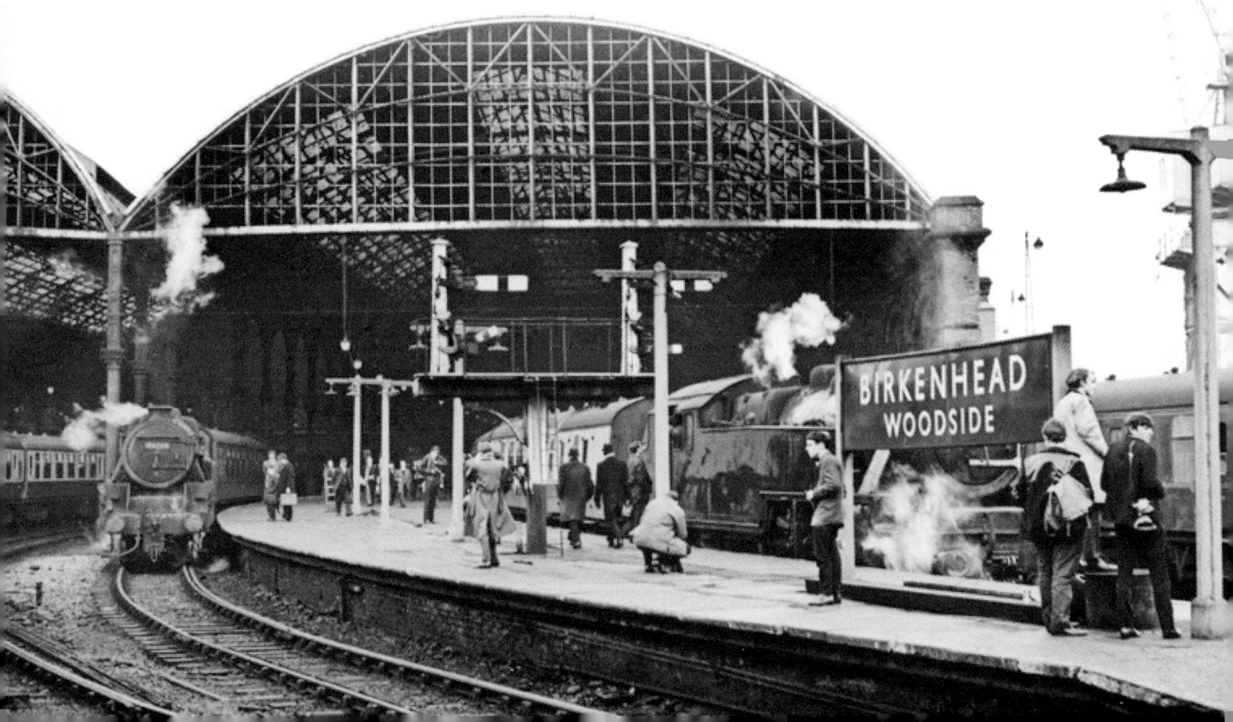

Helsby Branch
LITTLE SUTTON

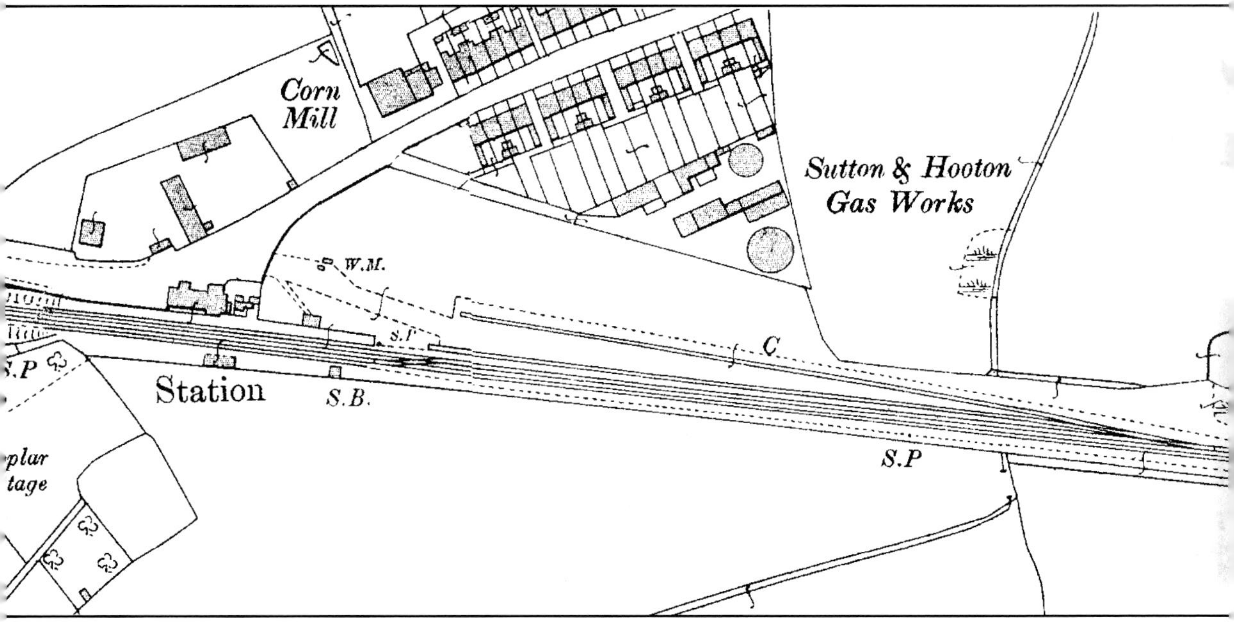

XIX. The 1911 survey includes a crane; this was of 3-ton capacity. The number of residents was 1109 in 1901 and 6958 in 1961.

95. An eastward view in about 1907 shows that the footbridge was yet to come, but that gas lighting had arrived. The gasworks was adjacent to the yard. The word LITTLE was added on 19th October 1886. (Stations UK)

96. Looking in the other direction in August 1960, we see a fresh signal box. It was in use until 9th September 1972 and the goods yard functioned until 31st March 1969, although it handled only coal after November 1965. (H.C.Casserley)

97. No. 508134 is working the 10.47 Liverpool Moorfields to Ellesmere Port on 9th March 2002. Remarkably, the building had retained its fine finials and ornate chimney pots, although the lad seems to have other interests. (P.D.Shannon)

OVERPOOL

98. The station opened on 15th August 1988 to serve new housing developments and electrification arrived in 1994. The photograph is from 2011. (Merseyrail)

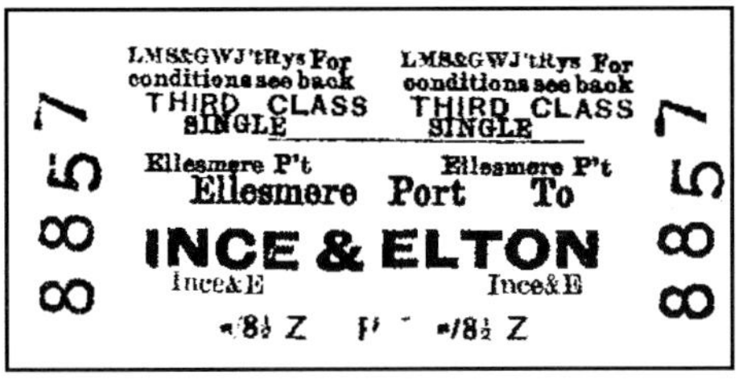

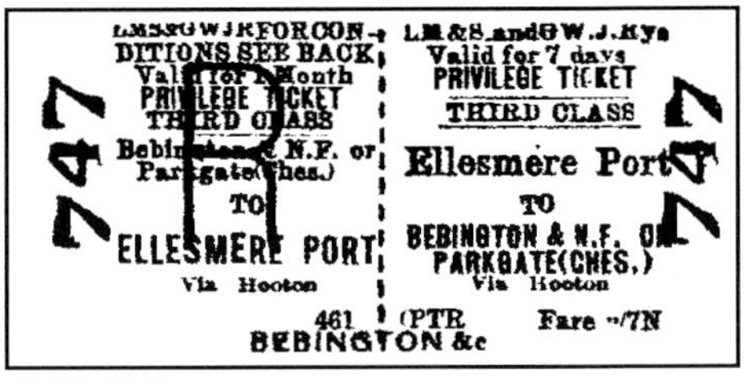

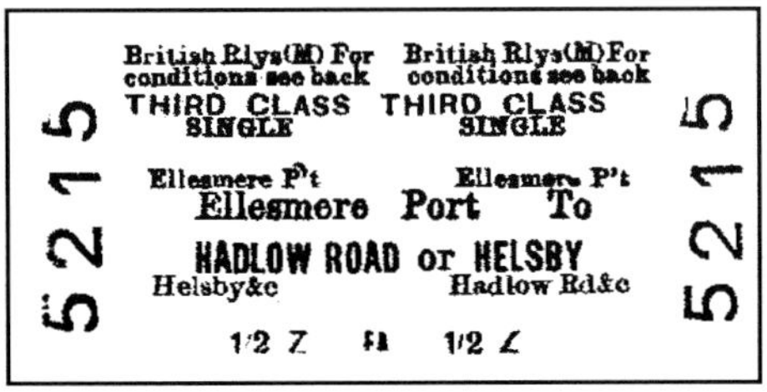

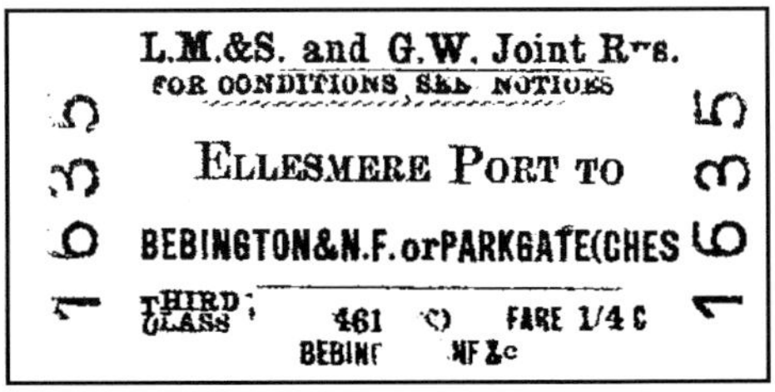

ELLESMERE PORT

99. A train bound for Helsby runs over the level crossing and passes near the crossing keepers hut and the engine shed. The map shows that the second coach is over the subway. There are varied goods items in transit. (Lens of Sutton coll.)

100. The LNWR sold its engine shed in 1921 to the MSC and some of its locomotives were recorded on 2nd July 1961. The canal was served by very extensive sidings belonging to the MSC. (R.S.Carpenter)

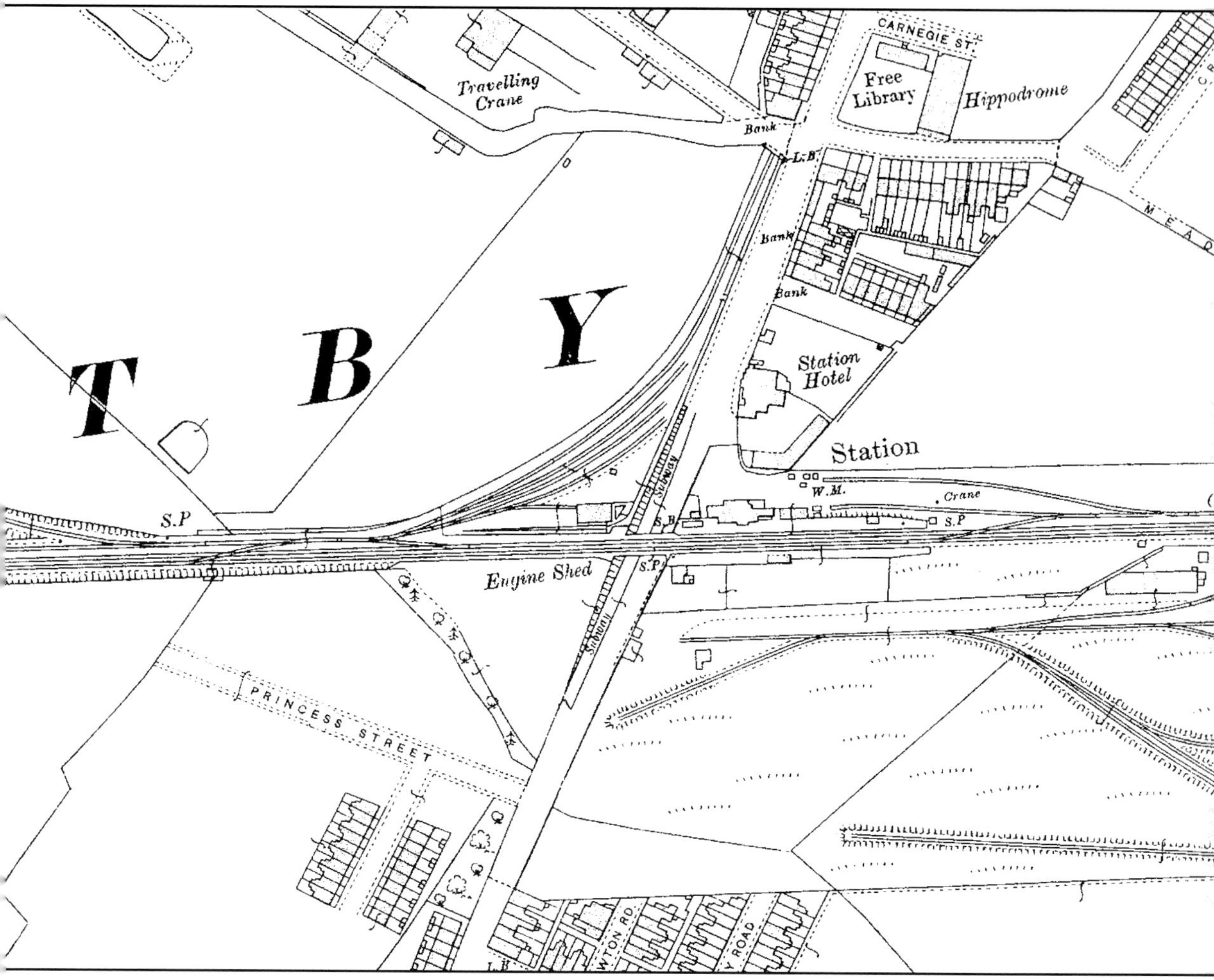

XX. The 1911 survey has the station and the LNWR engine shed on the left page. The line curving up on the left ran to various wharves on the Manchester Ship Canal and those on the right served diverse industries.

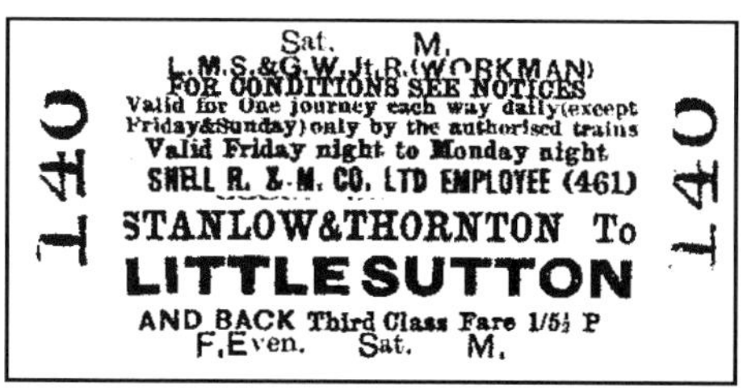
Sat. M.
L.M.S.&G.W.Jt.R.(WORKMAN)
FOR CONDITIONS SEE NOTICES
Valid for One journey each way daily(except Friday&Sunday) only by the authorised trains
Valid Friday night to Monday night
SHELL R. & M. CO. LTD EMPLOYEE (461)
140 STANLOW&THORNTON To 140
LITTLE SUTTON
AND BACK Third Class Fare 1/5½ P
F.Even. Sat. M.

Sat. M.
L.M.S.&G.W.Jt.R.(WORKMAN)
FOR CONDITIONS SEE NOTICES
Valid for One journey each way daily(except Friday&Sunday) only by the authorised trains
Valid Friday night to Monday night
SHELL R. & M. CO. LTD EMPLOYEE (461)
040 STANLOW&THORNTON To 040
MORETON
AND BACK Third Class Fare 3/8 P
F.Even. Sat. M.

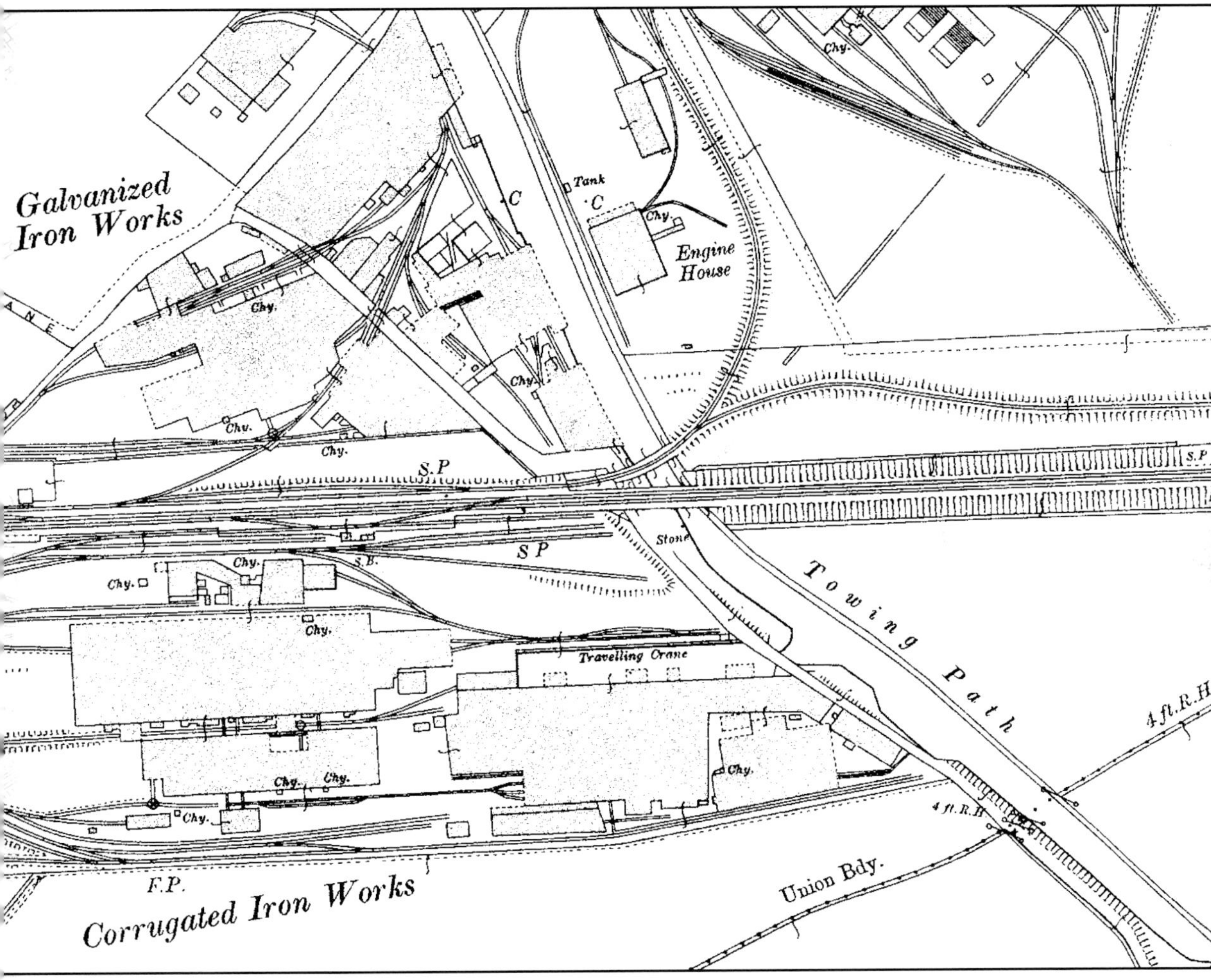
Galvanized
Iron Works
Chy.
Tank
C
Engine
House
S.P
S.B.
Stone
Towing Path
Travelling Crane
4 ft. R.H.
Union Bdy.
F.P.
Corrugated Iron Works

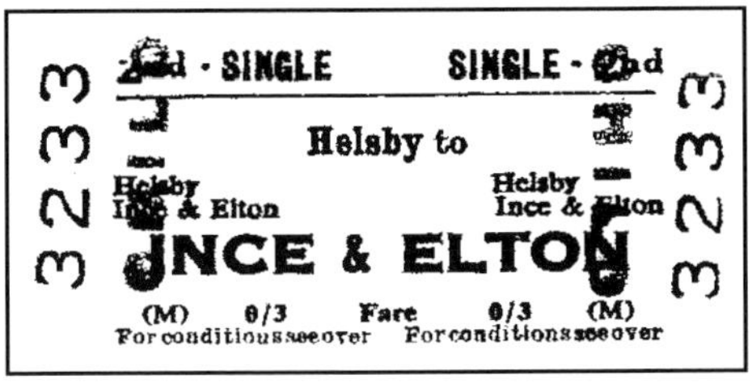
SINGLE
SINGLE
3233
3233
Helsby to
Helsby
Ince & Elton
Helsby
Ince &
INCE & ELTON
(M) 0/3 Fare 0/3 (M)
For conditions see over
For conditions see over

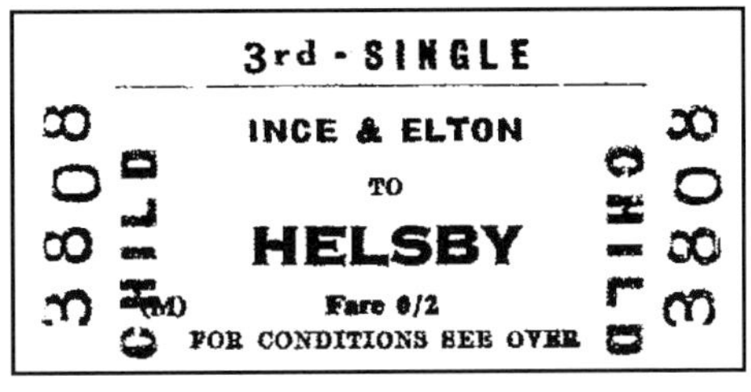
3rd - SINGLE
3808
3808
CHILD
CHILD
INCE & ELTON
TO
HELSBY
(M)
Fare 0/2
FOR CONDITIONS SEE OVER

101. No. 47123 is arriving from Hooton on 21st August 1984 with a train from Amlwch, which will soon terminate in the sidings of Associated Octel. The bridges were completed in 1960 and eliminated the level crossing. The goods yard had been north of the platforms until its closure on 20th July 1970. (D.H.Mitchell)

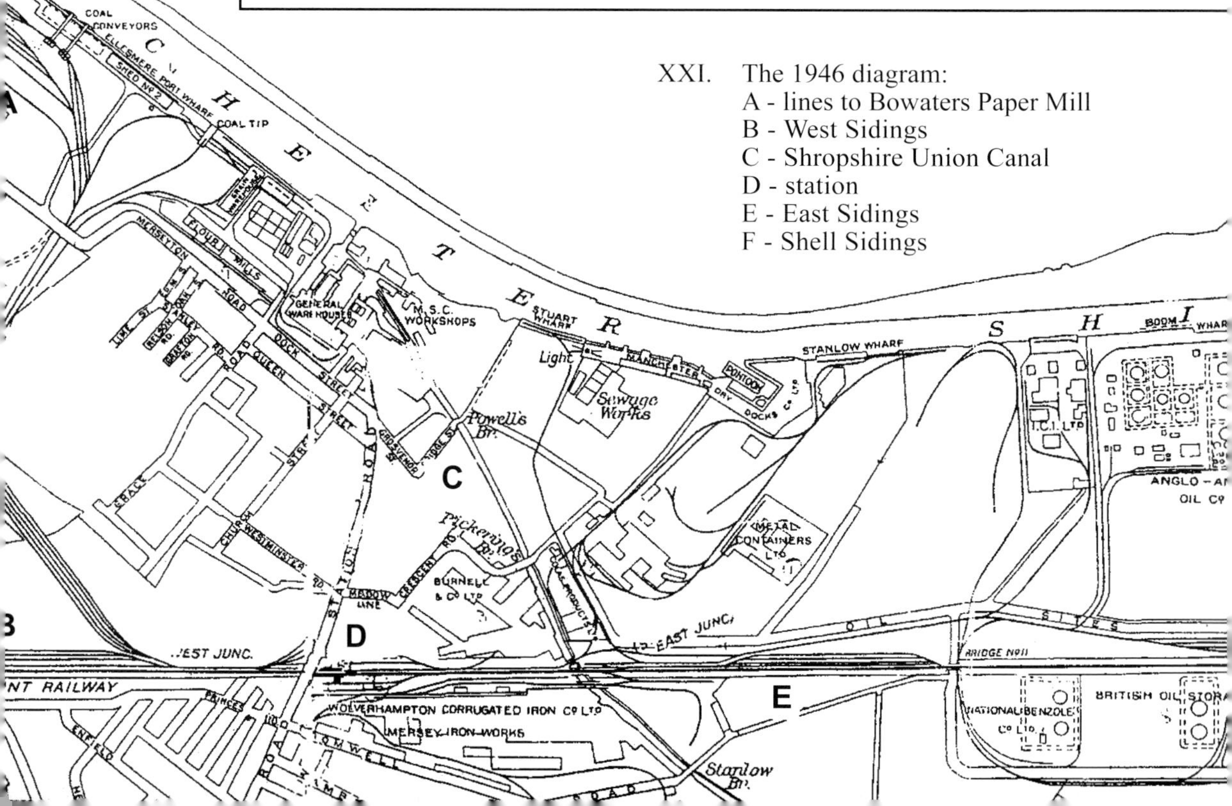

XXI. The 1946 diagram:
A - lines to Bowaters Paper Mill
B - West Sidings
C - Shropshire Union Canal
D - station
E - East Sidings
F - Shell Sidings

102. No. 08927 is shunting wagons, which have just arrived in the 13.00 from Warrington on 14th August 1986. The view east is from the bridge in the background of the next picture. (P.D.Shannon)

103. Electrification from Hooton to Ellesmere Port in 1994 left the route thence to Helsby something of a backwater and its passenger service was reduced from half hourly to four each way per day. Looking east from the footbridge, the 16.10 Merseyrail service to Liverpool Central and the 16.04 to Helsby will both depart wrong line after reversal. The date is 23rd July 2001 and no. 142028 is on the right, while no. 508138 stands on the eastern extremity of the conductor rail. The white building beyond the up platform is the 64-lever signal box. It was No. 4 when there were five boxes and it had a new upper structure following a fire in 1972. (A.C.Hartless)

STANLOW & THORNTON

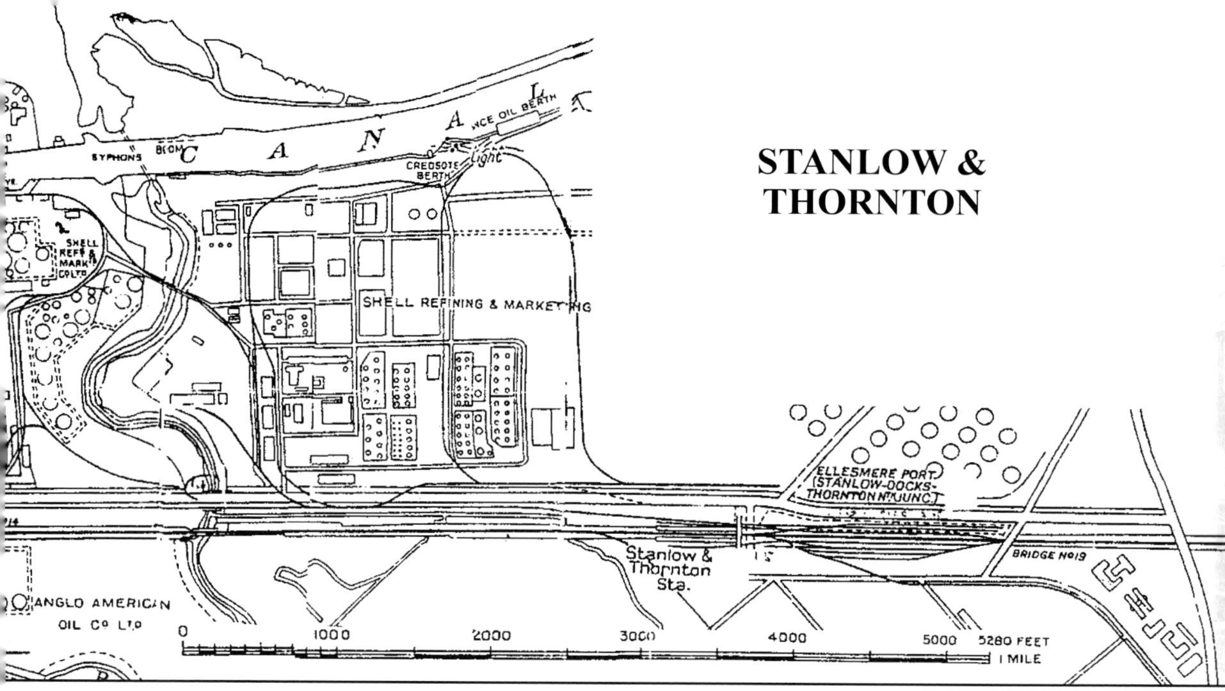

XXII. Continuation of the 1946 diagram. The area had developed greatly in the early 1940s, mainly to meet wartime fuel requirements. A bulk explosives storage depot was created, as were Royal Ordnance Factories, further south.

104. The station came into use for construction workers on 23rd December 1940 and opened to the public on 24th February 1941. The 15.36 Rock Ferry to Stanlow has just arrived on the left, while no. 40126 passes through with empty tankers on 19th September 1980. This locomotive gained fame in the Great Train Robbery. (T.Heavyside)

105. Few canal companies had such extensive lines to justify brake vans and shunting locomotives. Seen on 9th August 1982 is its Hudswell Clarke diesel, no. 3003. (D.H.Mitchell)

106. No. 25907 is working the 13.10 Warrington Arpley to Ellesmere Port on 14th August 1986. Near the end of the train is the 50-lever LMS signal box, which opened on 1st July 1940. It ceased to be used regularly in 1998 and closed on 11th February 2008. (P.D.Shannon)

107. The 13.49 Chester to Helsby was recorded on the same day, formed of M51185 and M54352. The station could have been described as "flat pack", but the term had not been invented. The platform on the right takes eight coaches, but the other will only accept seven. (P.D.Shannon)

108. Many of the bridges carried pipes, not people. On the left of this view from the footbridge are the Shell loading racks. No. 37418 is passing on 8th July 1991, with fuel oil for glass manufacture by Pilkingtons at Cowley Hill. (P.D.Shannon)

INCE & ELTON

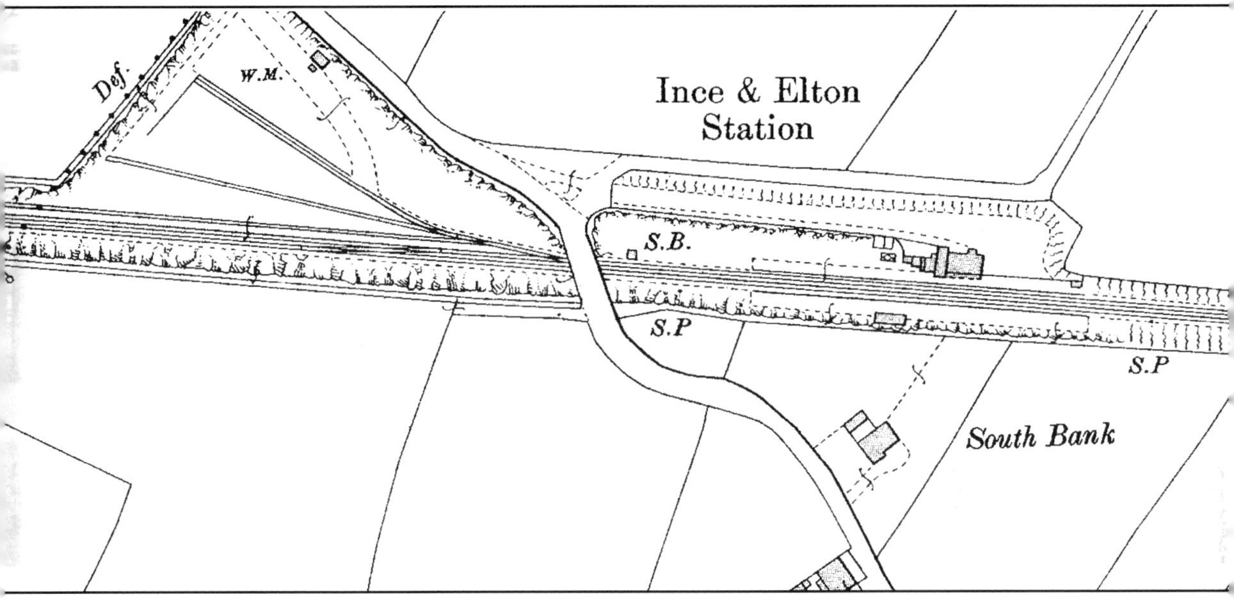

XXIII. The 1910 edition includes the goods yard, which was in use until 15th June 1961. The suffix had been added on 17th April 1884.

109. A GWR locomotive is seen westbound at the well kept station in a postcard view from about 1910. The card had faded badly. Ince is ½ mile northwest of the station and Elton developed southwest of it, but close by. (R.S.Carpenter coll.)

110. GWR 2-6-2T no. 5137 is pictured eastbound in September 1936. The ground had to be excavated for the station approach, on the right. The station was still devoid of a footbridge in 2012. (D.K.Jones coll.)

111. This panorama is from 1971 and we look towards Helsby. The platforms would accommodate four cars, but passengers had to cross on track level between them. The signal box had been in the left foreground, but closed on 12th April 1964. (Stations UK)

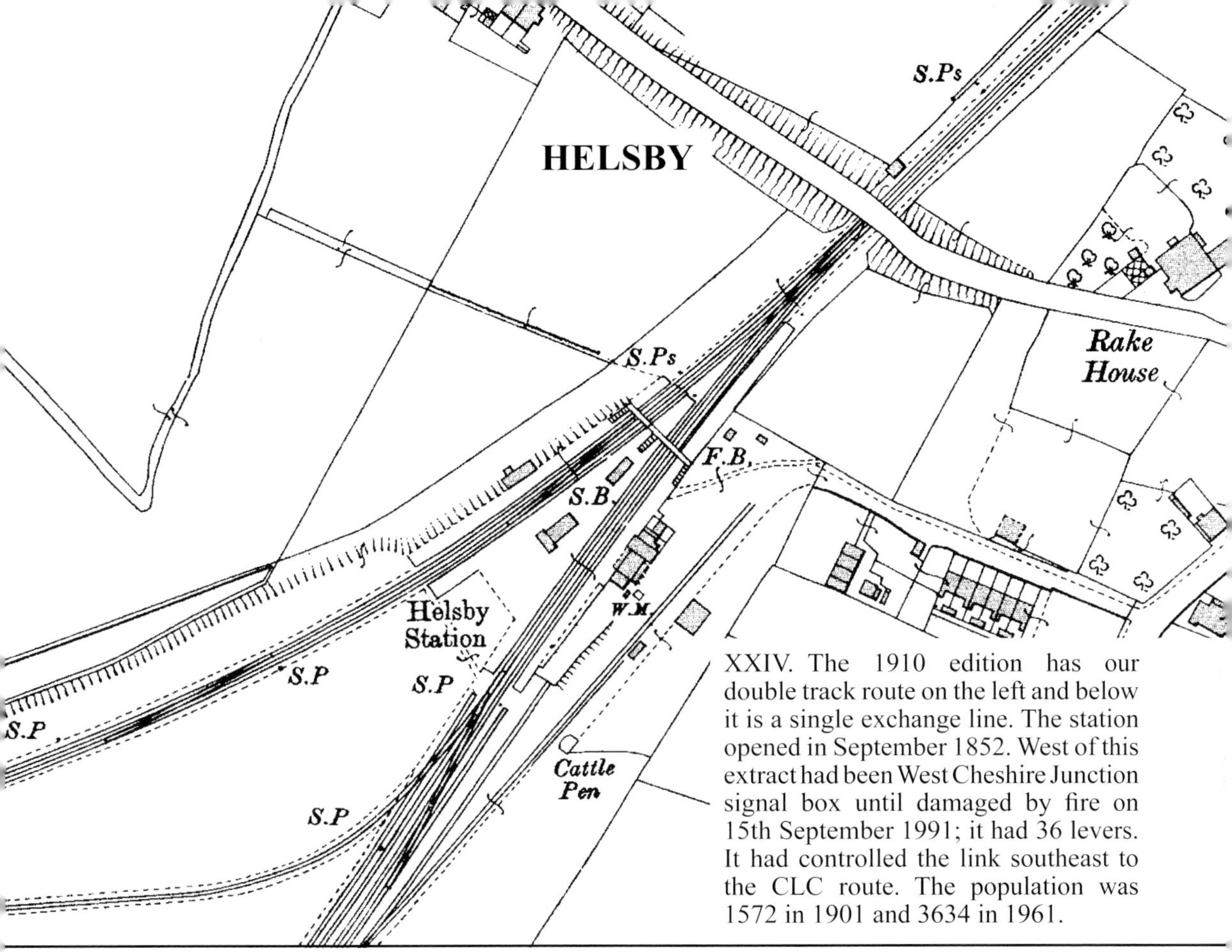

XXIV. The 1910 edition has our double track route on the left and below it is a single exchange line. The station opened in September 1852. West of this extract had been West Cheshire Junction signal box until damaged by fire on 15th September 1991; it had 36 levers. It had controlled the link southeast to the CLC route. The population was 1572 in 1901 and 3634 in 1961.

112. An outside-framed GWR 0-6-0 is signalled onto the main line in about 1908. Note its massive dome and short train. (R.S.Carpenter coll.)

113. The late afternoon sun was ideal to photograph 2-6-2T no. 40121 waiting to leave with the 5.22pm to Birkenhead Woodside on 7th August 1954. The footbridge had received roofing since the previous view. (H.Ballantyne)

114. It is 10th October 1959 and this panorama includes a push-pull train bound for Hooton propelled by class 2MT 2-6-2T no. 84000, a type introduced in 1953. It was the first one of the class. (H.C.Casserley)

115. The other end of the same train is seen before it is propelled out at 2.5pm. Some fine chimney stacks and finials can be enjoyed. (H.C.Casserley)

116. The east elevation and the long siding, together with an end loading dock, were photographed on 26th November 1964. Goods traffic ceased here on 3rd February 1964; the yard had a 5-ton crane recorded in 1938, when a siding was listed for the British Handle Company. (R.J.Essery/R.S.Carpenter coll.)

117. No. 40172 throbs gently as it takes the curve from Ince on 19th September 1980, bound for Warrington. One can continue to marvel at the architectural detailing. (T.Heavyside)

118. The footbridge roof had gone, but many people still changed trains here. Seen on 17th August 1984 is the 08.54 Manchester Victoria to Llandudno (left) and the 09.58 Helsby to Hooton. (D.H.Mitchell)

119. With only four axles, Pacer no. 142052 will soon bounce off to Chester, reversing at Hooton. Known as Skippers, the low seat backs gave a good view. There were several sidings in the right distance for Kemira Fertilisers; they branched off at Helsby Junction. (T.Heavyside)

120. The 15.48 Helsby to Ellesmere Port was worked by no. 150137 on 13th February 2002. Ten years later, a moderate service was still provided and the 45-lever signal box from 1900 was still in use. (P.D.Shannon)

MP Middleton Press
EVOLVING THE ULTIMATE RAIL ENCYCLOPEDIA
Easebourne Lane, Midhurst, West Sussex.
GU29 9AZ Tel:01730 813169
www.middletonpress.co.uk email:info@middletonpress.co.uk
A-978 0 906520 B- 978 1 873793 C- 978 1 901706 D-978 1 904474
E - 978 1 906008 F - 978 1 908174

All titles listed below were in print at time of publication - please check current availability by looking at our website - *www.middletonpress.co.uk* or by requesting a Brochure which includes our *LATEST* RAILWAY TITLES also our TRAMWAY, TROLLEYBUS, MILITARY and WATERWAYS series

A
Abergavenny to Merthyr C 91 8
Abertillery & Ebbw Vale Lines D 84 5
Aberystwyth to Carmarthen E 90 1
Allhallows - Branch Line to A 62 8
Alton - Branch Lines to A 11 6
Andover to Southampton A 82 6
Ascot - Branch Lines around A 64 2
Ashburton - Branch Line to B 95 4
Ashford - Steam to Eurostar B 67 1
Ashford to Dover A 48 2
Austrian Narrow Gauge D 04 3
Avonmouth - BL around D 42 5
Aylesbury to Rugby D 91 3
B
Baker Street to Uxbridge D 90 6
Bala to Llandudno E 87 1
Banbury to Birmingham D 27 2
Banbury to Cheltenham E 63 5
Bangor to Holyhead F 01 7
Bangor to Portmadoc E 72 7
Barking to Southend C 80 2
Barmouth to Pwllheli E 53 6
Barry - Branch Lines around D 50 0
Bath Green Park to Bristol C 36 9
Bath to Evercreech Junction A 60 4
Beamish 40 years on rails E94 9
Bedford to Wellingborough D 31 9
Birmingham to Wolverhampton E253
Bletchley to Cambridge D 94 4
Bletchley to Rugby E 07 9
Bodmin - Branch Lines around B 83 1
Bournemouth to Evercreech Jn A 46 8
Bournemouth to Weymouth A 57 4
Bradshaw's Guide 1866 F 05 5
Bradshaw's History F18 5
Bradshaw's Rail Times 1850 F 13 0
Bradshaw's Rail Times 1895 F 11 6
Branch Lines series - see town names
Brecon to Neath D 43 2
Brecon to Newport D 16 6
Brecon to Newtown E 06 2
Brighton to Eastbourne A 16 1
Brighton to Worthing A 03 1
Bromley South to Rochester B 23 7
Bromsgrove to Birmingham D 87 6
Bromsgrove to Gloucester D 73 9
Broxbourne to Cambridge F16 1
Brunel - A railtour D 74 6
Bude - Branch Line to B 29 9
Burnham to Evercreech Jn B 68 0
C
Cambridge to Ely D 55 5
Canterbury - BLs around B 58 9
Cardiff to Dowlais (Cae Harris) E 47 5
Cardiff to Pontypridd E 95 6
Cardiff to Swansea E 42 0
Carlisle to Hawick E 85 7
Carmarthen to Fishguard E 66 6
Caterham & Tattenham Corner B251
Central & Southern Spain NG E 91 8
Chard and Yeovil - BLs a C 30 7
Charing Cross to Dartford A 75 8
Charing Cross to Orpington A 96 3
Cheddar - Branch Line to B 90 9
Cheltenham to Andover C 43 7
Cheltenham to Redditch D 81 4
Chester to Birkenhead F 21 5
Chester to Rhyl E 93 2
Chichester to Portsmouth A 14 7
Clacton and Walton - BLs to F 04 8
Clapham Jn to Beckenham Jn B 36 7
Cleobury Mortimer - BLs a E 18 5
Clevedon & Portishead - BLs to D180
Colonel Stephens - His Empire D 62 3
Consett to South Shields E 57 4
Cornwall Narrow Gauge D 56 2
Corris and Vale of Rheidol E 65 9
Craven Arms to Llandeilo E 35 2
Craven Arms to Wellington E 33 8
Crawley to Littlehampton A 34 5
Cromer - Branch Lines around C 26 0
Croydon to East Grinstead B 48 0
Crystal Palace & Catford Loop B 87 1
Cyprus Narrow Gauge E 13 0
D
Darjeeling Revisited F 09 3
Darlington Leamside Newcastle E 28 4
Darlington to Newcastle D 98 2
Dartford to Sittingbourne B 34 3
Derwent Valley - BL to the D 06 7
Devon Narrow Gauge E 09 3
Didcot to Banbury D 02 9
Didcot to Swindon C 84 0
Didcot to Winchester C 13 0
Dorset & Somerset NG D 76 0
Douglas - Laxey - Ramsey E 75 8
Douglas to Peel C 88 8
Douglas to Port Erin C 55 0
Douglas to Ramsey D 39 5
Dover to Ramsgate A 78 9
Dublin Northwards in 1950s E 31 4
Dunstable - Branch Lines to E 27 7
E
Ealing to Slough C 42 0
East Cornwall Mineral Railways D 22 7
East Croydon to Three Bridges A 53 6
Eastern Spain Narrow Gauge E 56 7
East Grinstead - BLs to A 07 9
East London - Branch Lines of C 44 4
East London Line B 80 0
East of Norwich - Branch Lines E 69 7
Effingham Junction - BLs a A 74 1
Ely to Norwich C 90 1
Enfield Town & Palace Gates D 32 6
Epsom to Horsham A 30 7
Eritrean Narrow Gauge E 38 3
Euston to Harrow & Wealdstone C 89 5
Exeter to Barnstaple B 15 2
Exeter to Newton Abbot C 49 9
Exeter to Tavistock B 69 5
Exmouth - Branch Lines to B 00 8
F
Fairford - Branch Line to A 52 9
Falmouth, Helston & St. Ives C 74 1
Fareham to Salisbury A 67 3
Faversham to Dover B 05 3
Felixstowe & Aldeburgh - BL to D 20 3
Fenchurch Street to Barking C 20 8
Festiniog - 50 yrs of enterprise C 83 3
Festiniog 1946-55 E 01 7
Festiniog in the Fifties B 68 8
Festiniog in the Sixties B 91 6
Finsbury Park to Alexandra Pal C 02 8
Frome to Bristol B 77 0
G
Gloucester to Bristol D 35 7
Gloucester to Cardiff D 66 1
Gosport - Branch Lines around A 36 9
Greece Narrow Gauge D 72 2
H
Hampshire Narrow Gauge D 36 4
Harrow to Watford D 14 2
Harwich & Hadleigh - BLs to F 02 4
Hastings to Ashford A 37 6
Hawkhurst - Branch Line to A 66 6
Hayling - Branch Line to A 12 3
Hay-on-Wye - BL around D 92 0
Haywards Heath to Seaford A 28 4
Hemel Hempstead - BLs to D 88 3
Henley, Windsor & Marlow - BLa C77 2
Hereford to Newport D 54 8
Hertford & Hatfield - BLs a E 58 1
Hertford Loop E 71 0
Hexham to Carlisle D 75 3
Hexham to Hawick F 08 6
Hitchin to Peterborough D 07 4
Holborn Viaduct to Lewisham A 81 9
Horsham - Branch Lines to A 02 4
Huntingdon - Branch Line to A 93 2
I
Ilford to Shenfield C 97 0
Ilfracombe - Branch Line to B 21 3
Industrial Rlys of the South East A 09 3
Ipswich to Saxmundham C 41 3
Isle of Wight Lines - 50 yrs C 12 3
Italy Narrow Gauge F 17 8
K
Kent Narrow Gauge C 45 1
Kidderminster to Shrewsbury E 10 9
Kingsbridge - Branch Line to C 98 7
Kings Cross to Potters Bar E 62 8
Kingston & Hounslow Loops A 83 3
Kingswear - Branch Line to C 17 8
L
Lambourn - Branch Line to C 70 3
Launceston & Princetown - BLs C 19 2
Lewisham to Dartford A 92 5
Lines around Wimbledon B 75 6
Liverpool Street to Chingford D 01 2
Liverpool Street to Ilford C 34 5
Llandeilo to Swansea E 46 8
London Bridge to Addiscombe B 20 6
London Bridge to East Croydon A 58 1
Longmoor - Branch Lines to A 41 3
Looe - Branch Line to C 22 2
Lowestoft - BLs around E 40 6
Ludlow to Hereford E 14 7
Lydney - Branch Lines around E 26 0
Lyme Regis - Branch Line to A 45 1
Lynton - Branch Line to B 04 6
M
Machynlleth to Barmouth E 54 3
Maesteg and Tondu Lines E 06 2
March - Branch Lines around B 09 1
Marylebone to Rickmansworth D 49 4
Melton Constable to Yarmouth Bch E031
Midhurst - Branch Lines of E 78 9
Midhurst - Branch Lines to F 00 0
Mitcham Junction Lines B 01 5
Mitchell & company C 59 8
Monmouth - Branch Lines to E 20 8
Monmouthshire Eastern Valleys D 71 5
Moretonhampstead - BL to C 27 7
Moreton-in-Marsh to Worcester D 26 5
Mountain Ash to Neath D 80 7
N
Newbury to Westbury C 66 6
Newcastle to Hexham D 69 2
Newport (IOW) - Branch Lines to A 26 0
Newquay - Branch Lines to C 71 0
Newton Abbot to Plymouth C 60 4
Newtown to Aberystwyth E 41 3
North East German NG D 44 9
Northern France Narrow Gauge C 75 8
Northern Spain Narrow Gauge E 83 3
North London Line B 94 7
North Woolwich - BLs around C 65 9
O
Ongar - Branch Line to E 05 5
Oswestry - Branch Lines around E 60 4
Oswestry to Whitchurch E 81 9
Oxford to Bletchley D 57 9
Oxford to Moreton-in-Marsh D 15 9
P
Paddington to Ealing C 37 6
Paddington to Princes Risborough C819
Padstow - Branch Line to B 54 1
Peterborough to Kings Lynn E 32 1
Plymouth - BLs around B 98 5
Plymouth to St. Austell C 63 5
Pontypool to Mountain Ash D 65 4
Pontypridd to Merthyr F 14 7
Pontypridd to Port Talbot E 86 4
Porthmadog 1954-94 - BLa B 31 2
Portmadoc 1923-46 - BLa B 13 8
Portsmouth to Southampton A 31 4
Portugal Narrow Gauge E 67 3
Potters Bar to Cambridge D 70 8
Princes Risborough - BL to D 05 0
Princes Risborough to Banbury C 85 7
R
Reading to Basingstoke B 27 5
Reading to Didcot C 79 6
Reading to Guildford A 47 5
Redhill to Ashford A 73 4
Return to Blaenau 1970-82 C 64 2
Rhyl to Bangor F 15 4
Rhymney & New Tredegar Lines E 48 2
Rickmansworth to Aylesbury D 61 6
Romania & Bulgaria NG E 23 9
Romneyrail C 32 1
Ross-on-Wye - BLs around E 30 7
Ruabon to Barmouth E 84 0
Rugby to Birmingham E 37 6
Rugby to Loughborough F 12 3
Rugby to Stafford F 07 9
Ryde to Ventnor A 19 2
S
Salisbury to Westbury B 39 8
Saxmundham to Yarmouth C 69 7
Saxony Narrow Gauge D 47 0
Seaton & Sidmouth - BLs to A 95 6
Selsey - Branch Line to A 04 8
Sheerness - Branch Line to B 16 2
Shenfield to Ipswich E 96 3
Shrewsbury - Branch Line to A 86 4
Shrewsbury to Chester E 70 3
Shrewsbury to Ludlow E 21 5
Shrewsbury to Newtown E 29 1
Sierra Leone Narrow Gauge D 28 9
Sirhowy Valley Line E 12 3
Sittingbourne to Ramsgate A 90 1
Slough to Newbury C 56 7
South African Two-foot gauge E 51 2
Southampton to Bournemouth A 42 0
Southend & Southminster BLs E 76 5
Southern France Narrow Gauge C 47 5
South London Line B 46 6
South Lynn to Norwich City F 03 1
Southwold - Branch Line to A 15 4
Spalding - Branch Lines around E 52 9
St Albans to Bedford D 08 1
St. Austell to Penzance C 67 3
ST Isle of Wight A 56 7
Stourbridge to Wolverhampton E 16
St. Pancras to Barking D 68 5
St. Pancras to Folkestone E 88 8
St. Pancras to St. Albans C 78 9
Stratford-u-Avon to Birmingham D77
Stratford-u-Avon to Cheltenham C25
ST West Hants A 69 7
Sudbury - Branch Lines to F 19 2
Surrey Narrow Gauge C 87 1
Sussex Narrow Gauge C 68 0
Swanley to Ashford B 45 9
Swansea to Carmarthen E 59 8
Swindon to Bristol C 96 3
Swindon to Gloucester D 46 3
Swindon to Newport D 30 2
Swiss Narrow Gauge C 94 9
T
Talyllyn 60 E 98 7
Taunton to Barnstaple B 60 2
Taunton to Exeter C 82 6
Tavistock to Plymouth B 88 6
Tenterden - Branch Line to A 21 5
Three Bridges to Brighton A 35 2
Tilbury Loop C 86 4
Tiverton - BLs around C 62 8
Tivetshall to Beccles D 41 8
Tonbridge to Hastings A 44 4
Torrington - Branch Lines to B 37 4
Towcester - BLs around E 39 0
Tunbridge Wells BLs A 32 1
U
Upwell - Branch Line to B 64 0
V
Victoria to Bromley South A 98 7
Vivarais Revisited E 08 6
W
Wantage - Branch Line to D 25 8
Wareham to Swanage 50 yrs D098
Waterloo to Windsor A 54 3
Waterloo to Woking A 38 3
Watford to Leighton Buzzard D 45 6
Welshpool to Llanfair E 49 9
Wenford Bridge to Fowey C 09 3
Westbury to Bath B 55 8
Westbury to Taunton C 76 5
West Cornwall Mineral Rlys D 48 7
West Croydon to Epsom B 08 4
West German Narrow Gauge D 93 7
West London - BLs of C 50 5
West London Line B 84 8
West Wiltshire - BLs of D 12 8
Weymouth - BLs A 65 9
Willesden Jn to Richmond B 71 8
Wimbledon to Beckenham C 58 1
Wimbledon to Epsom B 62 6
Wimborne - BLs around A 97 0
Wisbech - BLs around C 01 7
Witham & Kelvedon - BLs a E 82 6
Woking to Alton A 59 8
Woking to Portsmouth A 25 3
Woking to Southampton A 55 0
Wolverhampton to Shrewsbury E444
Worcester to Birmingham D 97 5
Worcester to Hereford D 38 8
Worthing to Chichester A 06 2
Y
Yeovil - 50 yrs change C 38 3
Yeovil to Dorchester A 76 5
Yeovil to Exeter A 91 8
York to Scarborough F 23 9